MW01062609

Especially for

....

From

....

Date

....

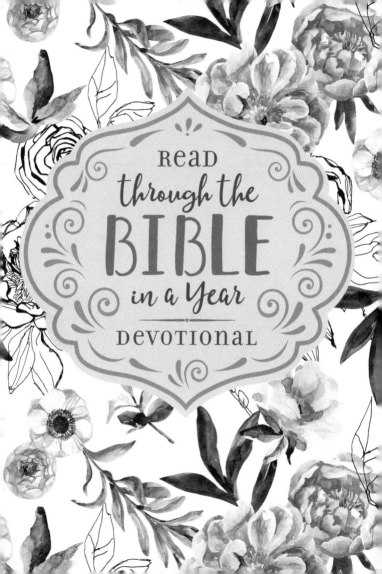

READ
through the
BIBLE
in a Year
DEVOTIONAL

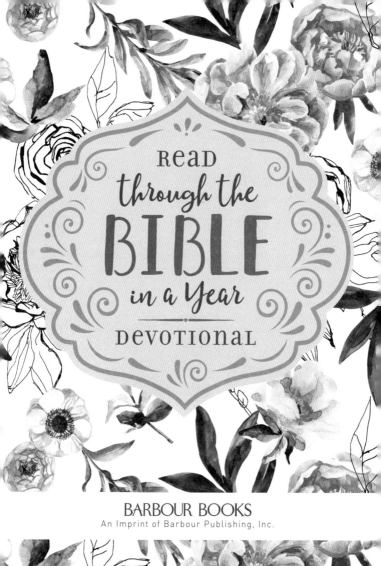

READ through the BIBLE in a Year

DEVOTIONAL

BARBOUR BOOKS
An Imprint of Barbour Publishing, Inc.

Our mission is to inspire the world with the life-changing message of the Bible.

 Member of the
Evangelical Christian
Publishers Association

Introduction

G od's Word is life giving (Matthew 4:4), true (Psalm 33:4), powerful (Hebrews 4:12), inspired by God (2 Timothy 3:16), profitable to equip and train you (2 Timothy 3:16–17), a light to show you your way (Psalm 119:105), a guide for a pure life (Psalm 119:9), everlasting (Isaiah 40:8; Matthew 24:35), wisdom giving (Proverbs 2:6), freeing (John 8:32), sustaining (Deuteronomy 8:3), able to save your soul (James 1:21), and something that will give you hope (Psalm 119:114; Psalm 130:5). God asks you to meditate on this precious gift and to make it a central part of your life. And He promises that if you do, He will make your way prosperous and successful (Joshua 1:8). As one of God's children, you simply cannot ignore His Word. The more intimately you know the Bible, the more fully you will come to know and love the Author. Look forward to how God will change your life as you read through and meditate on His Word this year.

*I*n this first reading of the year, we get a glimpse into the beautiful story that is woven throughout scripture. Genesis 1 speaks of the perfect world that God created. Psalm 1 is written in a fallen world that is marred by sin where we must actively avoid wickedness and seek purity. Matthew 1 is the beginning of God redeeming His people by sending His Son as one of us. Christ's very lineage is strewn with the aroma of redemption. His ancestors include such redeemed sinners as the harlot Rahab, the incestuous Judah and Tamar, the pagan Ruth, and the adulterous David and Bathsheba. God makes it no secret that His business is to redeem sinners and to show His power through the unlikely and the weak.

Day 1

GENESIS 1–2
MATTHEW 1
PSALM 1

And God saw every thing that he had made, and, behold, it was very good. And the evening and the morning were the sixth day.
GENESIS 1:31

Day 2

*G*enesis 3 presents a grim outlook on the future of humanity. But even in the midst of this chaos, God assures the serpent that one will come to wage war against him. Then in Psalm 2 an anointed King is proclaimed as Ruler over all the earth. And finally in Matthew, we catch a glimpse of this King. Though He was still a young child, the magi recognized Him as the King who was anointed to reign over the nations. A beautiful story of redemption begins to unfold.

Yet have I set my king upon my holy hill of Zion.
I will declare the decree: the LORD hath said unto me,
Thou art my Son; this day have I begotten thee.
Ask of me, and I shall give thee the heathen
for thine inheritance, and the uttermost
parts of the earth for thy possession.

PSALM 2:6–8

The holiness of God is vividly and frighteningly displayed in the account of the flood. Tragically, God in His holiness could not look on the degradation and sin being practiced by those whom He created. The God we serve today is just as holy and just as incensed by sin, but mercifully, we have been saved from His just wrath through the sacrifice of Christ. Repent of your sins and rest in the knowledge of your forgiveness through Christ.

Day 3

GENESIS 5–7
MATTHEW 3
PSALM 3

And saying, Repent ye: for the kingdom of heaven is at hand.
MATTHEW 3:2

Day 4

GENESIS 8–10
MATTHEW 4
PSALM 4

*N*o amount of money, prestige, or security measures can make you truly safe. It is only in Christ that you can find genuine rest, knowing that you are cared for and loved by the Ruler of the universe. Your heavenly Father has secured your future—an eternity with Him. So sleep peacefully, knowing that nothing can touch you outside of His will. God is faithful to His Word and dearly loves His children.

*I will both lay me down in peace,
and sleep: for thou, LORD,
only makest me dwell
in safety.*

PSALM 4:8

*J*ust like David, pray with confidence that God will hear you and then eagerly watch for His answer. Start your day off in conversation with your Father. To actively enter into His presence in the morning will make you more aware of Him the rest of the day. Pray for the small things and the big things, knowing that not only will God listen to you, but He will also act on your behalf.

My voice shalt thou hear in the morning,
O LORD; in the morning will I
direct my prayer unto thee,
and will look up.
PSALM 5:3

Day 6

GENESIS 14–16
MATTHEW 5:21–48
PSALM 6

Do you have faith like Abraham, who believed God that his descendants would be as numerous as the stars of heaven when at the time he had no children? His wife was past the age of childbearing, and they certainly would have been past the point of hoping for such a miracle. He had no earthly evidence that would have made him think that he could have innumerable descendants. But his faith in God caused him to disregard earthly circumstances in favor of heavenly promises.

And he brought him forth abroad, and said, Look now toward heaven, and tell the stars, if thou be able to number them: and he said unto him, So shall thy seed be. And he believed in the LORD; and he counted it to him for righteousness.

GENESIS 15:5–6

H ow often do you fail to take God's promises seriously? Maybe you feel you're not worthy. Maybe deep down you just don't think that God cares enough to keep His promises to you. Or maybe your doubt lies in a lack of faith in His power—that perhaps He can't actually do what He says. Fortunately, our lack of faith does not affect God's faithfulness. God will always keep His promises, whether or not we initially believe it. He will prove Himself to you as He did to Sarah.

Therefore Sarah laughed within herself, saying, After I am waxed old shall I have pleasure, my lord being old also? And the LORD said unto Abraham, Wherefore did Sarah laugh, saying, Shall I of a surety bear a child, which am old? Is any thing too hard for the LORD? At the time appointed I will return unto thee, according to the time of life, and Sarah shall have a son.

GENESIS 18:12–14

Day 8

GENESIS 19–20
MATTHEW 6:19–34
PSALM 8

How would it affect your life if you truly understood how important you are to God? God perfectly cares for everything He has created, including sparrows and wildflowers (Matthew 6:26–30). As His child and image bearer, you are much more important to Him than flowers and birds. He, the Creator of every star in the sky, is mindful of you! You can trust that you have and will have all that you need under His protection.

When I consider thy heavens, the work of thy fingers, the moon and the stars, which thou hast ordained; what is man, that thou art mindful of him? and the son of man, that thou visitest him?

PSALM 8:3–4

*G*od spared Isaac, Abraham's son, and blessed Abraham for having the faith to trust God even in the most confusing and heartbreaking of circumstances. God did not spare His own Son and yet blessed us based on no merit of our own. God did indeed provide the sacrificial Lamb. We have every reason to trust God as Abraham did. He's more than proven Himself.

And Abraham said, My son, God will provide himself a lamb for a burnt offering: so they went both of them together.
GENESIS 22:8

Day 10

GENESIS 24

MATTHEW 7:12–29

PSALM 9:9–20

Take time to think back over the faithfulness of God in your life. Remember those times when even in the midst of your doubt or fear He showed Himself to you in powerful and visible ways. If you truly know the character and person of God, you will unequivocally, without hesitation, put your trust in Him because you know without a shadow of a doubt that He has never and will never forsake you.

And they that know thy name will put their trust in thee: for thou, LORD, hast not forsaken them that seek thee.

PSALM 9:10

*M*ay we have the same attitude as the leper—coming to God with nothing left to give, bowing before Him in full reliance that He is powerful enough to give us strength and make us well. This

leper understood that the healing of his infirmity relied completely on the grace of God. Knowing that God *could* heal him, he didn't demand Him to, beg Him to, or even argue with Him about why He should. Instead, he worshipped Christ by humbly acknowledging His power both to heal and to decide whether to heal. Sometimes we doubt God's power simply because He chooses not to display it in the way we wish He would. If only we would approach every prayer with the same humble and worshipful stance as the leper.

And, behold, there came a leper and
worshipped him, saying, Lord, if thou
wilt, thou canst make me clean.
MATTHEW 8:2

Day 12

GENESIS 27:1–28:9
MATTHEW 8:18–34
PSALM 10:12–18

When the darkness and insidious evil of the world seem so powerful, it is imperative that you remember that the One who calmed the wind and the waves is still the Ruler of this earth. He will one day vanquish evil for all eternity. He will judge the earth so that man may no longer oppress His image bearers. He will make all things right. You must hold fast to this truth so you won't lose hope.

To judge the fatherless and the oppressed, that the man of the earth may no more oppress.

PSALM 10:18

Scripture is laden with stories of the compassion of God. Just in today's reading we see that He loves the unloved (Leah), He sees those who feel invisible (the woman with the hemorrhage), He invites

the outcasts in (the sinners and tax collectors), and He heals the sick and needy (the synagogue official's daughter and the blind men). You serve a compassionate and loving God who does not overlook any of His children. He cares deeply for you.

But Jesus turned him about, and when he saw her, he said, Daughter, be of good comfort; thy faith hath made thee whole. And the woman was made whole from that hour.

MATTHEW 9:22

Day 14

The Lord sees your struggles and hears your groaning. Your prayers do not fall on deaf ears. God will act in His own perfect timing. God will arise to vindicate the injustices done to His people. If you are oppressed or treated unjustly, recognize that no matter what people may say about you, you are vindicated and justified by the ultimate judge. Doesn't your standing before Him matter infinitely more than your status here on earth?

For the oppression of the poor, for the sighing of the needy, now will I arise, saith the Lord; I will set him in safety from him that puffeth at him.

PSALM 12:5

*A*lthough Jacob's prayer in Genesis 32 was probably inspired more by fear than faith, we can emulate him in that he called to mind God's promises. When you're faced with a fearful situation, remember the promises that God has made to you and pray them back to Him. Although He certainly doesn't need to be reminded of the promises He has made, it will bless you to be reminded of them.

But I have trusted in thy mercy; my heart shall rejoice in thy salvation. I will sing unto the LORD, because he hath dealt bountifully with me.
PSALM 13:5–6

Day 16

GENESIS 32:22–34:31

MATTHEW 10:37–11:6

PSALM 14

It is essential that you remember the times in your life when God has shown Himself to you in special or significant ways. Unlike Jacob, you probably don't have a permanent limp to constantly remind you of your encounter with God. But nevertheless, it is important to remember and celebrate God's faithfulness so that in times of trial, when it can be easy to doubt God, you have something concrete to look back on to remind you of how He always cares for you.

And Jacob called the name of the place Peniel: for I have seen God face to face, and my life is preserved.

GENESIS 32:30

Psalm 15 gives a list of attributes of one who would be worthy to dwell with God. It concludes in asserting that the one who does these things will never be shaken. This is not to say that struggles and heartbreaks will not reach the righteous. But when you dwell with God, the struggles of this world will be insignificant compared to the beauty and glory of your God. Someone who is anchored to an immovable Rock is hard to shake.

Day 17

GENESIS 35–36
MATTHEW 11:7–24
PSALM 15

Lord, who shall abide in thy tabernacle?
who shall dwell in thy holy hill?...
He that doeth these things shall
never be moved.

PSALM 15:1, 5

Day 18

GENESIS 37–38

MATTHEW 11:25–30

PSALM 16

God will show you the path of life. Put Him before you in every decision of your life. If the decision seems too daunting, simply ask Him to reveal the next right step. Make your most urgent desire be to serve Him. You will find that He will guide, protect, and preserve you. The more closely you bind yourself to Him, the more clearly you will experience the fullness of joy available in His presence. He desires to give you pleasures forevermore.

Thou wilt shew me the path of life: in thy presence is fulness of joy; at thy right hand there are pleasures for evermore.

PSALM 16:11

You instinctively protect your eyes from harm. When startled, you blink. If something comes flying suddenly in your direction, you immediately shield your face. The apple of your eye is valuable; therefore, you protect it. God's children are like the apple of His eye—something precious that He has taken great pains to protect. He will never fail or cease to protect you. Rest securely in the shadow of His wings.

Keep me as the apple of the eye, hide me under the shadow of thy wings.

PSALM 17:8

Day 20

GENESIS 41
MATTHEW 12:30–50
PSALM 18:1–15

When you are honored and glorified on earth, use it as an opportunity to turn the eyes of those praising you to God. May everything that you do on earth be to His glory, for then you will be fulfilling your purpose in this life. True humility is recognizing that your achievements are owed to God and to what others have done to get you where you are. So direct the praise to God and to others—that's where it belongs.

And Joseph answered Pharaoh, saying,
It is not in me: God shall give
Pharaoh an answer of peace.
GENESIS 41:16

G od knows your future, for He planned it out before you were even born. So ask the One who already knows your path to light your candle and enlighten your darkness. He will give you enough illumination to guide your feet to the next step you should take.

For thou wilt light my candle:
the LORD my God will
enlighten my darkness.
PSALM 18:28

Day 22

GENESIS 44–45
MATTHEW 13:10–23
PSALM 18:30–50

Never assume that someone is unable to be transformed by God's grace. Based upon the remarkably cruel way they treated Joseph, it would be easy to think that his brothers were past saving. And yet, in Judah (one of the brothers who was part of the horrific plan to kill Joseph) we see a dim and imperfect but unmistakable picture of Christ—he was willing to sacrifice his own life for the sake of his younger brother. God can work in any life.

Now therefore, I pray thee, let thy servant abide instead of the lad a bondman to my lord; and let the lad go up with his brethren.

GENESIS 44:33

God's Word is perfect, sure, clean, pure, true, and righteous. It enlightens eyes, makes the simple wise, converts souls, brings joy, and is entirely trustworthy because it endures forever.

The words of God are far more valuable than gold. It makes sense, then, that great reward is to be found in following His commandments. With such treasure at your fingertips, why would you not immerse yourself in His Word every day?

More to be desired are they than gold, yea, than much fine gold: sweeter also than honey and the honeycomb. Moreover by them is thy servant warned: and in keeping of them there is great reward.

PSALM 19:10–11

Day 24

GENESIS 47:27–49:28
MATTHEW 13:44–58
PSALM 20

Psalm 20 is a beautiful psalm to pray over your life. David's petitions are saturated with the power and knowledge of victory. As someone who has the blessing of living after Christ has conquered death and evil, you can pray with even more confidence in God's victory. You can boast in the name of God for He will save and He will keep you from stumbling. Set up your banners in His name, proclaiming to the world that you are His and that it is His power at work in you.

Now know I that the LORD saveth his anointed; he will hear him from his holy heaven with the saving strength of his right hand.

PSALM 20:6

*A*s demonstrated in the account of the Hebrews in Egypt, God will often use suffering to increase His people. The very means that man uses as an attempt to snuff out God's children God uses to make them stronger. So when the suffering inflicted on God's people feels overwhelming, rejoice—knowing that through it God will work mightily, thwarting the arrogant plans of man.

But the more they afflicted them,
the more they multiplied and grew.
EXODUS 1:12

Day 26

The beautiful, unbreakable thread of God's sovereignty is woven all throughout history. In today's reading, God used an evil pharaoh, a brutal nationwide infanticide, a "chance" encounter with an Egyptian princess, and a murderer and coward named Moses to accomplish His purposes. Never imagine that a personal besetting sin, weakness, or difficult circumstance is out of God's will or too difficult for Him to use for His glory.

And God said unto Moses, I Am That I Am: and he said, Thus shalt thou say unto the children of Israel, I Am hath sent me unto you.

Exodus 3:14

*H*ow easily we forget God's power and His goodness. In his fear of speaking to the people, Moses failed to remember that it was God who made him and who could easily help him speak. In the pressure of feeding a crowd, the disciples quickly forgot the miracle that Jesus had already performed to feed thousands. What have you forgotten about God? What anxieties have taken root in your heart simply because you have failed to remember that God is powerful and that He loves you and will fulfill His will for your life?

Do ye not yet understand, neither remember the five loaves of the five thousand, and how many baskets ye took up? Neither the seven loaves of the four thousand, and how many baskets ye took up?

MATTHEW 16:9–10

Day 28

Exodus 5:22–7:24
Matthew 16:13–28
Psalm 23

Psalm 23 is such a familiar psalm, yet it is so profound and packed with remarkably comforting and empowering truths. Don't overlook the beauty of this little psalm. Similarly, in Matthew 16, don't discount the power of Jesus' promise "I will build my church"—a remarkably simple phrase that speaks of the power, victory, and sovereign plan of God. No earthly or spiritual power can stand in the way of the inevitable progress of Christ's Gospel. Take courage and find peace in this truth.

And I say also unto thee, That thou art Peter, and upon this rock I will build my church; and the gates of hell shall not prevail against it.

Matthew 16:18

God made the world and everything in it. He still sustains and controls the earth and all its inhabitants. He proved His power over His creation in the multiple plagues He brought down

on Egypt. This same God with the same amount of power still reigns today. He is to be feared. But, as one of His children, His power ought to give you comfort and courage because there is nothing in your life that He does not have control over.

The earth is the LORD's, and the fulness thereof; the world, and they that dwell therein.

PSALM 24:1

Day 30

EXODUS 10–11
MATTHEW 17:10–27
PSALM 25

The process of getting the Israelites out of Egypt was a painful one. God continued to harden Pharaoh's heart, which in turn caused him to oppress the Israelites more and more. In the midst of it all, it would have been difficult not to question what possible purpose God could have for putting His people through this. And yet, we can look back on it now and see that God's purposes were to free His people, to show His power and glory to a heathen nation, and to start His people on a journey to a beautiful land they could call their own. Worship in the midst of confusing and frightening circumstances, relying on God to use your suffering for His glory and for your good.

Go in unto Pharaoh: for I have hardened his heart, and the heart of his servants, that I might shew these my signs before him: and that thou mayest tell in the ears of thy son, and of thy son's son, what things I have wrought in Egypt, and my signs which I have done among them; that ye may know how that I am the LORD.

EXODUS 10:1–2

*A*re you as confident in your integrity as David was in his? Could you ask God to judge you with a clear conscience? This kind of confidence in your own innocence may seem impossible—and on your own, it is. But the blood of the Passover Lamb covers you so that you too can have confidence in the day of judgment.

Day 31

EXODUS 12
MATTHEW 18:1–20
PSALM 26

Judge me, O LORD; for I have walked in mine integrity: I have trusted also in the LORD; therefore I shall not slide.

PSALM 26:1

Day 32

EXODUS 13–14
MATTHEW 18:21–35
PSALM 27

*M*oses was confident that God would act on behalf of His people. He told the people to watch carefully because he knew that they would see their God's salvation that day. His faith in God's promise to deliver His people from Egypt was so secure that not even six hundred chariots of Egypt could shake his confidence. And God did not let him down. You serve the same promise-keeping, all-powerful God today. May your faith be as strong as the faith of Moses so that you too can stand firm, assured of God's salvation even in the face of overwhelming odds.

And Moses said unto the people, Fear ye not, stand still, and see the salvation of the LORD, which he will shew to you to day: for the Egyptians whom ye have seen to day, ye shall see them again no more for ever.

EXODUS 14:13

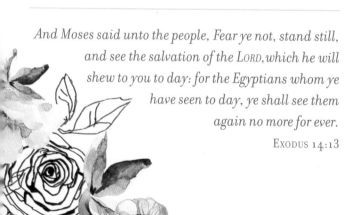

Psalm 28 provides us with a trustworthy equation: trust in God and you will be helped. Sometimes our prescription of the help we want God to provide is different from the help He does provide. But even though it may not feel like it in the moment, what God prescribes for you is infinitely better than anything you could imagine. Take a moment to recall times in your life when this has proven to be true. Then praise Him for His grace and faithfulness to you.

The LORD is my strength and my shield;
my heart trusted in him, and I am
helped: therefore my heart greatly
rejoiceth; and with my song
will I praise him.
PSALM 28:7

Day 34

EXODUS 17–19
MATTHEW 19:16–30
PSALM 29

Is there anything in your life that you would refuse to give up for the sake of Christ and His kingdom? The lack of ability to surrender possessions and earthly treasure to God is an indication that you have not fully known your God or the matchless riches that He offers to those who seek after Him. Jesus asks you to be willing to give up earthly comforts because He knows that what He can give is far better than anything this world can offer. It's only in letting go of earthly treasure that you can grab hold of Him.

Jesus said unto him, If thou wilt be perfect, go and sell that thou hast, and give to the poor, and thou shalt have treasure in heaven: and come and follow me.

MATTHEW 19:21

*H*ow easily we fall into questioning if God's plan for us is really the best. This doubt is often spurred on when we fall into the dangerous spiral of comparing our lives to the life of someone else. But since God is our Creator and Sustainer, doesn't He have the right to do with us as He pleases? More than that, doesn't He know best what is actually good for us? We must believe wholeheartedly in the goodness of God to protect ourselves from comparing our blessings to the blessings He's given others. There is beautiful freedom in truly accepting that God's treatment of you is perfect.

Is it not lawful for me to do what I will with mine own? Is thine eye evil, because I am good?
Matthew 20:15

Day 36

EXODUS 22–23
MATTHEW 20:20–34
PSALM 31:1–8

Though the laws of Exodus can sometimes seem tedious, God's character glimmers through in His instructions of how His people ought to live. His love and stalwart defense of the needy are seen in the recompense that He promises for anyone who dares afflict a widow or orphan. To take advantage of the weak and vulnerable is no small offense in God's eyes. God does not overlook those who are so often overlooked in our world—and, therefore, neither should we.

Ye shall not afflict any widow, or fatherless child. If thou afflict them in any wise, and they cry at all unto me, I will surely hear their cry; and my wrath shall wax hot, and I will kill you with the sword; and your wives shall be widows, and your children fatherless.

EXODUS 22:22–24

H ow would it change your life if you, like David, could truly grasp that your times are in God's hands? Wouldn't that belief foster an unshakable peace in your heart as it banishes fear from your life? You would know that the trials you go through are ordained by God and will be carefully worked out for your good. Why is it that we so often struggle to live our lives firmly planted in this truth?

My times are in thy hand: deliver me from the hand of mine enemies, and from them that persecute me.
PSALM 31:15

Day 38

Exodus 26–27
Matthew 21:28–46
Psalm 31:19–24

There is no deference to earthly status in the kingdom of God. All that matters is belief in the Son of God. Take this as an encouragement that no matter what you have done in this life, you are never past saving. And take it as a warning that no amount of good done in this life will get you into heaven apart from a saving knowledge of Christ.

Jesus saith unto them, Verily I say unto you,
That the publicans and the harlots go into
the kingdom of God before you.

Matthew 21:31

Those who trust in God are completely surrounded and encompassed by His mercy. It may be difficult to believe this in times when the hardships of life press so closely that they're almost suffocating. And yet, through all of life's struggles you have a layer of protection that can't be breached. Your life is completely in God's hands, and He will remain forever by your side.

Many sorrows shall be to the wicked:
but he that trusteth in the LORD,
mercy shall compass him about.
PSALM 32:10

Day 40

Exodus 29
Matthew 23:1–36
Psalm 33:1–12

Why does God command you to worship Him? Is it because He has some arrogant need to be noticed and praised? Not at all. If you were never to worship Him, it would not affect Him in the least. But it would affect you. Praising God is good, refreshing, and life giving for you. Don't neglect the wonderful gift of worshipping your God.

Rejoice in the Lord, O ye righteous: for praise is comely for the upright.

Psalm 33:1

W hat are you putting your trust in—status, money, health, strength, a good family? Psalm 33 reminds us that security comes from God and God alone. Set your trust on the Rock that will never move or crumble instead of on the shifting sands of the prosperity of this world.

There is no king saved by the multitude of an host:
a mighty man is not delivered by much strength.
An horse is a vain thing for safety: neither shall
he deliver any by his great strength. . . .
Our soul waiteth for the LORD: he is
our help and our shield.

PSALM 33:16–17, 20

Day 42

Do you spend more time trying to magnify yourself or striving to magnify God? In magnifying and exalting God there is great joy, as it brings you into closer relationship with Him. The more magnified God is in your life, the more perspective you will have regarding how small and insignificant you are. This in turn will inspire you to lean on Him, making you more powerful than you ever would be on your own. Surround yourself with people who are passionate about magnifying God as well.

O magnify the LORD with me,
and let us exalt his name together.

PSALM 34:3

*A*n encounter with God will inevitably change you. Just as the Israelites noticed that the face of Moses shone after meeting with God, so too when you commit to spending valuable time with God

each day, you will be changed in a noticeable and beautiful way. His glory will reflect off you, and His love will work through you.

And when Aaron and all the children of Israel saw Moses, behold, the skin of his face shone; and they were afraid to come nigh him.

Exodus 34:30

Day 44

Exodus 35:30–37:29
Matthew 25:14–30
Psalm 35:1–8

Our talents are God given. Therefore, don't derive arrogance from them, but instead humbly thank God for the skills He has given you. Conversely, don't allow yourself to belittle the gifts that God has given you. Joyfully and confidently use them for His service.

And he hath filled him with the spirit of God, in wisdom, in understanding, and in knowledge, and in all manner of workmanship.

Exodus 35:31

Good deeds are often unnoticed and without thanks in this life. Maybe you even wonder why you still go out of your way to help others. But even if the world doesn't notice, be confident that God notices all the times you reach out to someone in need. God will reward your good works. In fact, in doing good for others you will find yourself in a closer relationship with your God, for He says, "Inasmuch as ye have done it unto one of the least of these my brethren, ye have done it unto me."

Day 45

Exodus 38–39
Matthew 25:31–46
Psalm 35:9–17

And the King shall answer and say unto them, Verily I say unto you, Inasmuch as ye have done it unto one of the least of these my brethren, ye have done it unto me.

Matthew 25:40

Day 46

Exodus 40
Matthew 26:1–35
Psalm 35:18–28

*I*n the desert, the Israelites in a very tangible way had to rely on God for their next step. If the pillar of cloud or fire moved, they moved. If it stayed in place, they waited. We too are on a pilgrimage through this land and must rely on God's guidance for each next step. While we may wish that His presence were as obvious to us as it was to them, we have the greater blessing of having His indwelling Spirit to lead and to guide us. Wait and watch for His movements to guide you into the next phase of your service to Him.

And when the cloud was taken up from over the tabernacle, the children of Israel went onward in all their journeys: but if the cloud were not taken up, then they journeyed not till the day that it was taken up.

Exodus 40:36–37

It is uncomfortable and upsetting to read the account of how all of Jesus' disciples abandoned Him to a violent mob that would treat Him, the Son of God, with a callous and shameful arrogance. And yet, don't

we often treat Him in the same way? We fail to speak of Him at the first sign of opposition. We continually go back to the same sin as if to say that His sacrifice was not enough to save us. We move our time with Him to the lowest priority as though anything else in our life would be more important than time with our Savior. Repent of the arrogant ways that you have treated the Son of God.

But all this was done, that the scriptures of the prophets might be fulfilled. Then all the disciples forsook him, and fled.
MATTHEW 26:56

Day 48

Leviticus 4:1–5:13
Mt. 26:69–27:26
Psalm 36:7–12

The tainted money that Judas received for betraying Jesus was used to buy a field in which strangers would be buried. It is a testimony to the all-encompassing love of God that He caused even this filthy money to be used for good. The field bought by Jesus' blood was used to give a final resting place to those who otherwise would have had none. God can truly redeem even the most heinous of acts.

And the chief priests took the silver pieces, and said, It is not lawful for to put them into the treasury, because it is the price of blood. And they took counsel, and bought with them the potter's field, to bury strangers in.

Matthew 27:6–7

While on the cross, Christ asked why God had forsaken Him. In answer to that question, God could point to each of His children and say that it is for us that Christ was forsaken on the cross. This kind of love is unfathomable to us, that Christ would endure such pain for a people who would so easily abandon Him and spit in His face. He was forsaken so that we never would be. This is the kind of love that we should never take for granted and that should inspire in us worshipful gratefulness.

Day 49

LEVITICUS 5:14–7:21
MATTHEW 27:27–50
PSALM 37:1–6

And about the ninth hour Jesus cried with a loud voice, saying, Eli, Eli, lama sabachthani? that is to say, My God, my God, why hast thou forsaken me?

MATTHEW 27:46

Day 50

LEVITICUS 7:22–8:36
MATTHEW 27:51–66
PSALM 37:7–26

*G*od orders your steps and then delights to see you walking in them. What peace this affords, that God knows and lovingly controls all your decisions. And even when you stumble, you will not fall, because the almighty God is by your side to catch and uphold you.

The steps of a good man are ordered by the LORD: and he delighteth in his way. Though he fall, he shall not be utterly cast down: for the LORD upholdeth him with his hand.

PSALM 37:23–24

The reason that God's people are able to go out into the world to make disciples and bring the Gospel to every nation is because all authority has been given to Christ. This knowledge infuses courage into all evangelism. Christ has already won and sits victoriously on His throne and is with us always, even to the end of the world. He has already chosen out for Himself a people to be His. It is simply our responsibility to faithfully preach His Word. He has already taken care of the hard part.

And Jesus came and spake unto them, saying, All power is given unto me in heaven and in earth. Go ye therefore, and teach all nations, baptizing them in the name of the Father, and of the Son, and of the Holy Ghost: teaching them to observe all things whatsoever I have commanded you: and, lo, I am with you always, even unto the end of the world. Amen.

MATTHEW 28:18–20

Day 52

LEVITICUS 11–12
MARK 1:1–28
PSALM 38

Do you have the same confidence as David wrote about in this psalm that God will hear when you call to Him? Where is your hope? If it is in your own abilities or merit, then you will find yourself disappointed. Securely fasten your hope to God's love and care for you, and you will never be let down.

*For in thee, O LORD, do I
hope: thou wilt hear,
O Lord my God.*
PSALM 38:15

Pray that God would give you the eternal perspective of how short this life really is. How would it change your life if you knew how it would end? How differently would you live each day if you really understood how few days you had? We are only pilgrims on this earth. Use the short time here to do the greatest good for God's kingdom and for those around you.

LORD, make me to know mine end, and the measure of my days, what it is: that I may know how frail I am.

PSALM 39:4

Day 54

Leviticus 14
Mark 1:40–2:12
Psalm 40:1–8

*N*otice the beautiful juxtaposition in today's reading. The passage in Leviticus laboriously sets out how a leper ought to be treated and the intense work of cleansing that had to happen. The passage in Mark depicts Christ reaching out and touching a leper to instantly make him well. Touching a leper would have been unheard of in the old Law. But Christ came to usher in a new law in which He touches the unclean and invites the outcast in.

And Jesus, moved with compassion, put forth his hand, and touched him, and saith unto him, I will; be thou clean.

Mark 1:41

What a beautiful God we serve who would rather eat with sinners and outcasts than maintain His social standing in a crowd of hypocrites. If you ever find yourself becoming too concerned about your social image, just remember what kind of Savior you should be emulating.

And it came to pass, that, as Jesus sat at meat in his house, many publicans and sinners sat also together with Jesus and his disciples: for there were many, and they followed him.

MARK 2:15

Day 56

LEVITICUS 16–17
MARK 4:1–20
PSALM 41:1–4

Once a year the high priest would make atonement for all the people to cleanse them from their sins. But this cleansing would only cover the sins of one year. Now, what beautiful freedom we have that Christ's onetime work on the cross has and will cover all our sins for all time.

For on that day shall the priest make an atonement for you, to cleanse you, that ye may be clean from all your sins before the LORD.

LEVITICUS 16:30

The same God who controls the winds and the sea lives inside you today. Fear has no place and no power against such a formidable opponent. When it seems like the waves of life are threatening to take you under, remember who it is that reigns as King in your heart. Ask Him to still the fear in your life and grant you peace.

And he arose, and rebuked the wind, and said unto the sea, Peace, be still. And the wind ceased, and there was a great calm.
MARK 4:39

Day 58

Leviticus 20
Mark 5
Psalm 42–43

Christ radically changed the life of the woman in Mark 5 in more ways than one. First, He healed her bleeding. But perhaps even more importantly, He called her "daughter." This woman would have been an outcast in her society with little human contact because of her condition. So can you imagine the spiritual and emotional healing she must have felt at the hands of her Savior to have been called His daughter—a term of endearment and belonging? You also are called a child of God and forever belong to Him, no matter what happens on this earth.

And he said unto her, Daughter, thy faith hath made thee whole; go in peace, and be whole of thy plague.

MARK 5:34

Day 59

LEVITICUS 21–22
MARK 6:1–13
PSALM 44

N otice the refrain that often punctuates the end of a point of the Law through Leviticus—"I am the LORD." There didn't need to be any other justification for why the Israelites were to follow the laws set forth. There doesn't need to be any other justification for why we ought to follow the commands and guidance of God today. The fact that the One giving the commands is the perfectly holy, almighty God is reason enough to follow Him wholeheartedly.

Neither shall ye profane my holy name;
but I will be hallowed among the children
of Israel: I am the LORD which hallow
you, that brought you out of the land of
Egypt, to be your God: I am the LORD.
LEVITICUS 22:32–33

Day 60

LEVITICUS 23–24
MARK 6:14–29
PSALM 45:1–5

Though the laws in Leviticus may sometimes seem harsh and tedious, God put them in place for the good of His people. God instituted a Sabbath rest because He knew that as humans it is essential for our well-being to have a day to rest and recuperate. Do you honor this rest that God has given you? Trust God that He knows what is best for you and strive to joyfully keep the Sabbath.

Six days shall work be done: but the seventh day is the sabbath of rest, an holy convocation; ye shall do no work therein: it is the sabbath of the LORD in all your dwellings.

LEVITICUS 23:3

If you tend to feel guilty about taking time to rest in a world that demands so much action, take note that Jesus encouraged His disciples to rest from the trying work of evangelism. Seek out time to rest in God and to find rejuvenation in Him. Then go back out into the world refreshed and ready to continue His work.

*And he said unto them, Come ye yourselves
apart into a desert place, and rest a while:
for there were many coming and going,
and they had no leisure so much as to eat.*

MARK 6:31

Day 62

LEVITICUS 26
MARK 7
PSALM 45:13–17

*M*ay we not be the kind of people that God could say of, "[They] honoureth me with their lips, but their heart is far from me." Instead, ask God that your heart be so filled with love and adoration of Him that it would overflow into praise and service for His kingdom. May our actions prove our words to be true so that we can be faithful witnesses for Christ.

He answered and said unto them, Well hath Esaias prophesied of you hypocrites, as it is written, This people honoureth me with their lips, but their heart is far from me.

MARK 7:6

Psalm 46 is one of the most comforting psalms to meditate on in times of suffering. Even when the whole world seems to be coming apart at the seams, you have no reason to fear because God is with you and will never forsake you. Take a moment in the chaos of life to be still and dwell on the truths in this psalm. Know that He is God, that He is in complete control, and that He is your ever-present refuge and strength in times of trouble.

Be still, and know that I am God: I will be exalted among the heathen, I will be exalted in the earth. The LORD of hosts is with us; the God of Jacob is our refuge. Selah.

PSALM 46:10–11

Day 64

NUMBERS 1–2
MARK 9:1–13
PSALM 47

*A*long with the people in Psalm 47, you too can "shout unto God with the voice of triumph." Why? Because God has secured victory over the world, sin, and death. It may feel like the battle is still raging here on earth and in your own life. But in heaven the Victor, Christ, sits on His throne orchestrating all history under His reign. So shout for joy and rejoice in the victory that you have in Christ.

*O clap your hands, all ye people; shout
unto God with the voice of triumph.*

PSALM 47:1

It's often not until we reach rock bottom in our desperation that we truly understand how much we need God. It's in these moments of candid weakness and vulnerability that we can recognize how small we

are and how big God is. God also uses these times to show us how little we really know of Him. Notice how in Mark 9 Jesus doesn't heal the man's son right away. Instead, He waits until the man is entirely sure of his total need of Christ. He even needs help to believe. Don't be ashamed to ask God to help you believe in His love and power. It's through those times of deepest suffering that He lovingly draws you into a more intimate relationship with Him.

And straightway the father of the child
cried out, and said with tears, Lord,
I believe; help thou mine unbelief.

MARK 9:24

Day 66

NUMBERS 4

MARK 10:1–34

PSALM 48:9–14

It is a beautiful thing to serve a God who has lived on this earth as a human, has suffered temptation and loss, has died the death of a mortal, and has risen victorious over it all. There is nowhere you can go and nothing you can do that Christ won't be able to guide you through. Christ has even gone before you in death so that you need not fear that dreaded inevitability. He will hold your hand and walk you through into everlasting glory on the other side. He is your God forever and ever.

For this God is our God for ever and ever:
he will be our guide even unto death.

PSALM 48:14

*C*hrist turned the values and expectations of His society upside down. Instead of the conquering King that the Jews expected, the Messiah came as a lowly servant whose ultimate act on this earth was a cursed death. Instead of raising up an army of courageous men, Christ sought followers who would humbly serve others. His kingdom is one where the attitude of a child is honored and where weakness is used to greater advantage than strength. His ways are still countercultural and still capable of changing lives and moving mountains.

And whosoever of you will be the chiefest, shall be servant of all. For even the Son of man came not to be ministered unto, but to minister, and to give his life a ransom for many.

MARK 10:44–45

Day 68

Numbers 6:22–7:47

Mark 11

Psalm 49:10–20

For those who don't acknowledge Christ as Lord, there will always be a nagging feeling of meaninglessness and futility to life. They may try to ignore this feeling by building for themselves an empire here on earth or by drowning themselves in pleasure. And yet, that gnawing knowledge will always remain. But for those who are in Christ, a far greater reality awaits us than anything this earth can offer. Once our work here is done, the grave is only an entryway into the matchless glory that will receive us in heaven.

Like sheep they are laid in the grave; death shall feed on them; and the upright shall have dominion over them in the morning; and their beauty shall consume in the grave from their dwelling. But God will redeem my soul from the power of the grave: for he shall receive me. Selah.

Psalm 49:14–15

The nature of your relationship with God is one that can be hard to comprehend because it is like no other relationship that you have. There is literally nothing that you can offer God that He could not gain on His own. He owns the entire world. So many of our earthly relationships are based on what we can give and get. Our pride and self-sufficiency often leave us feeling uncomfortable if we believe that there is nothing we can give to a relationship. We like to be needed. But with God we have to lay the desire to be needed aside. All we can do is humbly give Him our service and praise.

If I were hungry, I would not tell thee: for the world is mine, and the fulness thereof. . . . Offer unto God thanksgiving; and pay thy vows unto the most High.

PSALM 50:12, 14

Day 70

Numbers 8:5–9:23
Mark 12:28–44
Psalm 50:16–23

The Israelites had to live day by day, watching and waiting for the cloud or pillar of fire to move from its place. Once the presence of God moved, they had to follow it without delay. Are you as willing to pack up your life and your comforts to follow God wherever He may lead? We would probably grumble and complain to be forced to live in such limbo. And yet, aren't we only sojourners and nomads on this earth? Beware of getting so attached to the things and places of this world that you would grumble to follow the pillar of fire wherever it may lead.

And so it was, when the cloud abode from even unto the morning, and that the cloud was taken up in the morning, then they journeyed: whether it was by day or by night that the cloud was taken up, they journeyed. Or whether it were two days, or a month, or a year, that the cloud tarried upon the tabernacle, remaining thereon, the children of Israel abode in their tents, and journeyed not: but when it was taken up, they journeyed.

Numbers 9:21–22

*I*n this psalm, David understood the true nature of sin. Every sin is an insult to God and grieves Him deeply. We are often so nonchalant with our sins, imagining that they are pretty much harmless. But Christ didn't die for something inconsequential and harmless. It is important to recognize the weight of each and every sin. Only when we see how abhorrent sin is can we truly come to appreciate the sacrifice Christ made for us.

Against thee, thee only, have I sinned,
and done this evil in thy sight:
that thou mightest be justified
when thou speakest, and be
clear when thou judgest.

PSALM 51:4

Day 72

NUMBERS 12–13
MARK 13:9–37
PSALM 51:10–19

A fascinating little phrase is tucked into Numbers 12:3—Moses was the meekest man on earth. At first this may seem surprising. Moses was, after all, the leader of a multitude of people, a direct correspondent with God, and someone who had performed miracles. But rather than making him arrogant, the fact that he had seen and spoken with God was the very thing that made him humble. Throughout the Bible an encounter with God never puffs up but inevitably brings people to their knees. Our smallness, inconsequence, and transience is recognized so much more clearly when seen in the radiance of the person of God. No wonder Moses was the meekest man on earth since he knew his God better than any man on earth.

(Now the man Moses was very meek, above all the men which were upon the face of the earth.)

NUMBERS 12:3

Joshua and Caleb had remarkable courage and faith. They believed in the power and faithfulness of God in spite of terrifying enemies and faithless, complaining friends. It would have been easy for them to have conformed to the crowd and sided with the majority. But they had enough faith in God to speak up against the majority. How often do we shy away from speaking up for our beliefs because we're scared? Or maybe we're just not fully convinced that He actually is a promise keeper. Fortunately, our faithlessness does not affect His faithfulness.

Day 73

NUMBERS 14
MARK 14:1–31
PSALM 52

If the LORD delight in us, then he will bring us into this land, and give it us; a land which floweth with milk and honey.
NUMBERS 14:8

Day 74

NUMBERS 15
MARK 14:32–72
PSALM 53

Psalm 53:1 says that they are fools who believe that there is no God. It seems that today's culture is increasingly asserting the belief that those who believe there *is* a God are the foolish ones. And yet, all creation points to a thoughtful, creative engineer. Could it really be that those who find a depth of peace beyond anything this world can offer, those who give their lives for the sake of others and their faith, those whose greatest desire is to please God. . .could it really be that they are the fools? No, those who deprive themselves of a life-giving relationship with God are truly the fools.

The fool hath said in his heart, There is no God. Corrupt are they, and have done abominable iniquity: there is none that doeth good.

PSALM 53:1

*J*esus could have silenced the taunts by coming down off the cross or by calling down legions of angels who would have shocked and awed His murderers. Though doing this would likely have converted much of the watching crowd, the story would have inevitably become legend after a few generations. Instead of saving Himself, Christ bore the shame, insults, and utter humiliation to become so much more than a legend. By keeping silent before His false accusers He became a Savior to everlasting generations. God so often doesn't use the flashy, eye-catching techniques we might use to accomplish His will. Instead, He uses the relentless endurance of His servants whose greatest desire is to have His will supersede their own. Christ was clearly the ultimate example of this.

Likewise also the chief priests mocking said among themselves with the scribes, He saved others; himself he cannot save.

MARK 15:31

Day 76

NUMBERS 17–18
MARK 15:33–47
PSALM 55

Joseph of Arimathaea was bold enough to align himself with the crucified King when he came to take His body for burial. When the majority of Christ's disciples were in hiding, Joseph was publicly honoring Jesus. This was a risky move on his part. He could have easily been ostracized or worse. But the impact that Christ had on him was great enough to overcome the fear of men. Would you be as bold to align yourself with Someone who was just killed by hateful mobs?

Joseph of Arimathaea, an honourable counsellor, which also waited for the kingdom of God, came, and went in boldly unto Pilate, and craved the body of Jesus.

MARK 15:43

*E*ven in His resurrection Christ was showing the world His heart for the weak and those without status. The first person He appeared to was not a chief priest or even one of the twelve disciples. He showed Himself first to a woman. In the culture of the day, women were not highly esteemed. But this woman loved her Savior enough to be the first one at the grave very early in the morning. The hearts of those who love Him are so much more precious to Christ than any earthly status.

Now when Jesus was risen early the first day of the week, he appeared first to Mary Magdalene, out of whom he had cast seven devils.

MARK 16:9

Day 78

Numbers 21:1–22:20
Luke 1:1–25
Psalm 56:8–13

Do you believe that God is for you? Or do you believe that maybe He likes you or at least tolerates you when you do what He wants? To believe that God is for you is to have an unshakable confidence that everything that happens in your life is orchestrated by God for your good and His glory. This certainly can be a hard thing to believe during times of personal struggles or heartbreak. But God is for you. And one day, in this life or the next, you'll be able to look back and see the beautiful tapestry that He's woven of your life where each thread of struggle leads to matchless joy.

When I cry unto thee, then shall mine enemies turn back: this I know; for God is for me.

PSALM 56:9

*Y*ou never know what seemingly frustrating thing in your life is actually God's way of saving you from harm. In the story of Balaam's donkey in Numbers 22, Balaam was angry at his donkey for continually turning away from the path. Most of us could easily put ourselves in his shoes with his anger building as things continued to not go his way. But the angel of the Lord eventually told him that the very thing he was angry about was what saved his life. An annoying, frustrating, or even very trying situation in life may just be God protecting and guiding you.

And the ass saw me, and turned from me
these three times: unless she had turned
from me, surely now also I had slain
thee, and saved her alive.
NUMBERS 22:33

Day 80

NUMBERS 24–25
LUKE 1:57–2:20
PSALM 58

God orchestrates history in such an exquisitely unique way. Centuries-old prophecies of a Messiah being born in Bethlehem were fulfilled because of the seemingly mundane act of having to travel for a census. The Savior of the world was born into a world that apparently had no room for Him, forcing Him to be born in a stable. Shepherds, a very lowly class in their culture, were the first to enter the courts of the King. Given the opportunity, it's doubtful that any of us would have written the story of the most important birth in history this way. But in that is the awesome beauty of it all. This is not a man-made story; this is the story of the Creator and Sustainer of the universe.

And she brought forth her firstborn son, and wrapped him in swaddling clothes, and laid him in a manger; because there was no room for them in the inn.

LUKE 2:7

*G*od gave His servant Simeon a marvelous blessing to allow him to see the Messiah before he died. Simeon understood the prophecies and plan of God and recognized Jesus for what He was—

Day 81

NUMBERS 26:1–27:11
LUKE 2:21–38
PSALM 59:1–8

God's salvation to Israel and the Gentiles. How glorious that he could behold the Savior who would soon bring to fruition all the promises of God that Simeon knew and held to as his hope.

Lord, now lettest thou thy servant depart in peace, according to thy word: for mine eyes have seen thy salvation, which thou hast prepared before the face of all people; a light to lighten the Gentiles, and the glory of thy people Israel.

LUKE 2:29–32

Day 82

How often do you openly praise God for His power and mercy? He sustains us every day of our lives, and yet we sometimes fail to acknowledge that. We often struggle to praise Him privately in our own hearts for all He's done for us, let alone proclaim aloud His praise to others. No matter what happens in your life, you still have ample reason to praise God at the end of the day.

But I will sing of thy power; yea, I will sing aloud of thy mercy in the morning: for thou hast been my defence and refuge in the day of my trouble.

PSALM 59:16

What a splendid and inexplicable mystery it is that Jesus was both fully man and fully God when He came to earth. He had a traceable genealogy. He came from a line of humans from which He would have inherited strengths, weaknesses, and physical traits. When God chose to come to earth to dwell among men, He didn't show up with a fancy entrance or a doting entourage proclaiming His deity. Instead, He chose to come as part of a family.

Which was the son of Enos, which was the son of Seth, which was the son of Adam, which was the son of God.
LUKE 3:38

Day 84

Numbers 31
Luke 4
Psalm 60:6–12

Where do you turn first when you are struggling with something? Have you ever had the experience where you realize hours after anxiously working through a problem that you still haven't asked the Lord for help? In this psalm, we're told that the help of man is vain. Your only completely trustworthy source of help is your heavenly Father. While He can (and does) graciously use the people around you to give you sound wisdom and advice, you should still always turn to Him before anyone else with your troubles.

Give us help from trouble: for vain is the help of man. Through God we shall do valiantly: for he it is that shall tread down our enemies.

PSALM 60:11–12

Peter truly understood his standing before God. In Luke 5:8, he is so aware of his sinfulness and Jesus' holiness that he asks that Jesus would depart from him. Are we as aware of how filthy our sins are in the light of God's perfection? Or do we generally think we have it pretty well together?

When Simon Peter saw it, he fell down at Jesus' knees, saying, Depart from me; for I am a sinful man, O Lord.
LUKE 5:8

Day 86

NUMBERS 34–36
LUKE 5:17–32
PSALM 62:1–6

David understood that with God as his refuge he could not be moved. He calls God his rock. This would not have meant a stone or even a boulder but rather a mountain. Just as mountains are unshakably solid, so is God for those who seek refuge in Him. Run to the Rock and hide yourself in His shadow.

He only is my rock and my
salvation: he is my defence;
I shall not be moved.

PSALM 62:6

*M*oses rebukes the people for not believing God about the land He had promised them. This was the God who had dwelled with them for the entire journey, showing them the way in a cloud

by day and as their light at night. This was the God who had proven Himself over and over again. And yet, they chose fear instead of faith. Is your first reaction to a difficult situation fear or faith? Hasn't God "proven" Himself to you as well?

Yet in this thing ye did not believe the Lord your God, who went in the way before you, to search you out a place to pitch your tents in, in fire by night, to shew you by what way ye should go, and in a cloud by day.

Deuteronomy 1:32–33

Day 88

DEUT. 2:26–4:14

LUKE 6:12–35

PSALM 63:1–5

*E*arthly success is not at all synonymous with spiritual success. In His sermon, Jesus called those who are poor, hungry, weeping, and hated by men blessed—hardly attributes that we would use to describe a "successful" life. If someone doesn't fit into our nicely defined version of earthly success, it does not in any way mean that God is not blessing that person. So much can be learned from passionate followers of Christ who use their poverty, hunger, sorrow, and persecution for the glory of their God.

And he lifted up his eyes on his disciples,
and said, Blessed be ye poor: for
yours is the kingdom of God.

LUKE 6:20

od is not a God who makes Himself hard to find. He does not try to hide Himself from us or veil Himself so that we can't know Him. In times when God seems far off or it feels like He's abandoned you, maybe you have not been seeking Him as you need to. He promises to be found by those who seek Him—therefore, you have a 100 percent chance of success when searching to know God.

But if from thence thou shalt seek the LORD thy God, thou shalt find him, if thou seek him with all thy heart and with all thy soul.
DEUTERONOMY 4:29

Day 90

Deut. 5:23–7:26
Luke 7:1–17
Psalm 64:1–5

*C*hrist's ministry is defined by so much compassion. His actions were inspired not by a people-pleasing, surface-level compassion but a deep-seated love for people, even people that He didn't know. Pray that God would instill in you the same kind of compassion that Christ so beautifully displayed. In this passage, Jesus very dramatically changed the life of this woman, but even a small act of compassion and kindness has the power to turn a life around.

Now when he came nigh to the gate of the city, behold, there was a dead man carried out, the only son of his mother, and she was a widow: and much people of the city was with her. And when the Lord saw her, he had compassion on her, and said unto her, Weep not.

Luke 7:12–13

$\mathcal{M}$oses called the people to remember—to remember their trying journey through the wilderness. They were to remember the humbling times, the proving grounds, and the heart-revealing struggles. They were to remember that God was leading them through those times every step of the way. It is a worthwhile endeavor to record the paths that God has led you down. Remember how faithfully He has led you so that you can boldly step into the future, entrusting yourself to Him as your guide.

And thou shalt remember all the way which the LORD thy God led thee these forty years in the wilderness, to humble thee, and to prove thee, to know what was in thine heart, whether thou wouldest keep his commandments, or no.

Deuteronomy 8:2

Day 92

DEUTERONOMY 10–11
LUKE 7:36–8:3
PSALM 65:1–8

The irony of Luke 7:39 is almost comic. In his heart the Pharisee was scoffing at Jesus for not knowing that the woman who was showering Him with honor was a sinner. Meanwhile, Jesus not only knew exactly what this woman had done in the past and the repentance that was now in her heart, but He also knew the disrespectful thoughts that the Pharisee was thinking. The Pharisee had grossly underestimated the insight and power of the Man he was dining with.

Now when the Pharisee which had bidden him saw it, he spake within himself, saying, This man, if he were a prophet, would have known who and what manner of woman this is that toucheth him: for she is a sinner.

LUKE 7:39

*H*ave you ever been outside on one of those days where you can almost hear nature praising its Maker? Have you ever seen a sight so heart-wrenchingly gorgeous that you have to start praising Him as well? What a wonderful thing that God has so blessed us by putting His beauty and creativity on full display for our pleasure. May we never take His creation for granted.

They drop upon the pastures of the wilderness:
and the little hills rejoice on every side.
The pastures are clothed with flocks;
the valleys also are covered over with
corn; they shout for joy, they also sing.
PSALM 65:12–13

Day 94

DEUT. 14:1–16:8
LUKE 8:22–39
PSALM 66:1–7

Are you ever surprised when God does something amazing in your life? The disciples in today's passage were in fearful awe when Jesus calmed the wind and the waves. Christ rebuked them, asking, "Where is your faith?" Why is it that we are sometimes surprised when we see God's goodness in our lives? Is our faith so weak or our knowledge of God so limited that we doubt His power and love?

And he said unto them, Where is your faith? And they being afraid wondered, saying one to another, What manner of man is this! for he commandeth even the winds and water, and they obey him.

LUKE 8:25

Today's passage in Luke is a lovely example of how God uses both miraculous and ordinary means to complete His work. Jesus miraculously healed the girl, but then He instructed her parents to give her something to eat. This seems like an oddly mundane thing to instruct them to do after He just performed the phenomenal feat of bringing her back from the dead. But we shouldn't be surprised when God uses ordinary means to advance His kingdom.

And her spirit came again, and she arose straightway: and he commanded to give her meat.

LUKE 8:55

Day 96

DEUT. 19:1–21:9
LUKE 9:1–22
PSALM 66:16–20

Though the majority of us aren't facing enemy armies on a daily basis, we still have battles to fight nearly every day. Some may be more difficult than others, but we all at some point need courage to face the next step in life. Go forward with confidence knowing that it is God who fights for you. Fear not, for the all-powerful God is on your side.

And shall say unto them, Hear, O Israel, ye approach this day unto battle against your enemies: let not your hearts faint, fear not, and do not tremble, neither be ye terrified because of them; for the LORD your God is he that goeth with you, to fight for you against your enemies, to save you.

DEUTERONOMY 20:3–4

We all certainly want God to bless us. But why do we want Him to bless us? Merely for our own good, comfort, or security? In today's psalm, the author asked to be blessed so that others may

know of the greatness of God. Use the blessings that God has bestowed on you to talk of and magnify Him. Strive to always be enthusiastic to speak of God and all that He has done for you so that others may be blessed by Him as well.

God be merciful unto us, and bless us;
and cause his face to shine upon us;
Selah. That thy way may be known
upon earth, thy saving health
among all nations.

PSALM 67:1–2

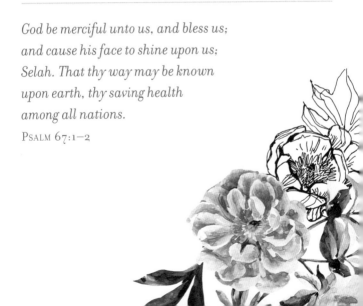

Day 98

Deut. 23:9–25:19
Luke 9:43–62
Psalm 68:1–6

God is a relational God. So much so that even in His own person He is not one but three. It's no wonder, then, that He feels so strongly for the orphan, the widow, and those who don't belong anywhere. His heart for these people is so apparent throughout all of scripture. He is the Father to those who have none and the protector of the widow. He places those without a home into families. If God is so concerned about these children of His, shouldn't we be as well? And in times when you feel as though you don't belong anywhere, remember that God is always by your side as your loving Father.

A father of the fatherless, and a judge of the widows, is God in his holy habitation. God setteth the solitary in families: he bringeth out those which are bound with chains: but there bellious dwell in a dry land.

PSALM 68:5–6

*J*esus presents an interesting challenge in today's passage. He adjured the disciples to rejoice not in the power that they had through Him, but in the fact that their names were written in the Book of Life. How often do we rejoice in earthly pursuits or successes and forget that the single most important thing for which to be grateful is our salvation? While we absolutely should rejoice in the gifts that God has given us on earth, it would benefit us to think more often on the greatest gift of all that God has given us—eternal life through His Son.

Notwithstanding in this rejoice not, that the spirits are subject unto you; but rather rejoice, because your names are written in heaven.

Luke 10:20

Day 100

Deut. 28:15–68
Luke 10:21–37
Psalm 68:15–19

The Lord "daily loadeth us with benefits." What marvelous imagery that is. It implies that the blessings that God gives us on a daily basis are so bountiful as to almost be too much to carry. Our lives are overflowing with the goodness of God. Take a moment to ponder and write down some of the benefits that God has given you in the past week.

Blessed be the Lord, who daily loadeth us with benefits, even the God of our salvation. Selah.

Psalm 68:19

*J*ust like the Israelites, every day we are faced with a choice: Will we choose death and a curse or life and a blessing? The choice seems simple enough—as Moses said, choose life. And yet, don't we often choose death when we continually go back to old patterns of sinful thought or behavior? We purposefully neglect our life-giving time with God for other worthless pursuits. Think about ways in which you can choose life on a daily basis, and then wait for the beautiful ways in which God will pour that abundant life into you.

Day 101

DEUTERONOMY 29–30
LUKE 10:38–11:23
PSALM 68:20–27

I call heaven and earth to record this day against
you, that I have set before you life and death,
blessing and cursing: therefore choose life,
that both thou and thy seed may live.

DEUTERONOMY 30:19

Day 102

DEUT. 31:1–32:22
LUKE 11:24–36
PSALM 68:28–35

*M*oses spoke such beautiful words to the Israelites before his death. He encouraged them to be courageous because God would go with them and would never fail or forsake them. You serve the same God today. He will never fail you, forsake you, or leave your side. How can you be confident that this is true? Because He forsook His own Son so that He would never have to turn His face from you. What a humbling and glorious truth. There is no one who can be trusted more fully than a God who has sacrificed so much to redeem you. So be courageous. Your God will never fail or forsake you.

Be strong and of a good courage, fear not, nor be afraid of them: for the LORD thy God, he it is that doth go with thee; he will not fail thee, nor forsake thee.

DEUTERONOMY 31:6

The Bible is an incredibly relatable book. It's filled with stories of people we can relate to—it's not filled with stories of perfect human beings whose faith is so strong that they never struggle or doubt God. Psalm 69 is just one example of a child of God in deep, overwhelming turmoil. Don't ever be afraid or ashamed to cry out to God in this way. Your faith or standing with Him is not lessened because you feel like the waters are encompassing you and you desperately need His help. Take courage from these very real humans in the Bible and speak to God with as much candor as they did.

*Save me, O God; for the waters
are come in unto my soul.*

PSALM 69:1

Day 104

*L*uke 12:4–5 may sound like a threat at first. But in these words of Christ's is actually glorious comfort. In the whole scheme of eternity, we really have nothing to fear from man. And for those who are in Christ, we have nothing to fear from God because we have already been adopted into His family and redeemed for eternal life in heaven. Therefore, we have nothing to fear at all because, in the end, all man can do is hasten us on to a beautiful eternity with God in glory.

And I say unto you my friends, Be not afraid of them that kill the body, and after that have no more that they can do. But I will forewarn you whom ye shall fear: Fear him, which after he hath killed hath power to cast into hell; yea, I say unto you, Fear him.

LUKE 12:4–5

The faith of Joshua in this verse is so inspiring. He didn't tell the people to sanctify themselves just in case God decided to do something amazing. He didn't tell the people to hope and pray that God would show up. No, he told them to sanctify themselves because God will do wonders tomorrow. There is no doubting or second-guessing. Joshua knew his God. He knew Him to be an absolutely faithful promise keeper.

Day 105

JOSHUA 3:1–5:12
LUKE 12:16–40
PSALM 69:18–28

And Joshua said unto the people,
Sanctify yourselves: for to morrow the
LORD will do wonders among you.
JOSHUA 3:5

Day 106

Joshua 5:13–7:26

Luke 12:41–48

Psalm 69:29–36

Do you live every day in anticipation of Christ's coming? Or do you put off ministry and service for God's kingdom, reasoning that you'll do that when you have more time in the future? Our time on earth is the only chance we'll get to share Christ with others. It's the only chance we have to serve the needy and hurting. Don't wait for this time to pass. Live for Christ's kingdom and His coming today and every day.

Blessed is that servant, whom his lord
when he cometh shall find so doing.

Luke 12:43

*C*hrist told His disciples that He did not come to bring peace but division. This is not exactly a heartwarming concept. But it can certainly be encouraging for you if you are facing opposition simply

because you align yourself with Christ. Christ promised that where He was and where He was proclaimed there would be resistance. Sometimes facing opposition for the sake of Christ is a sign that you are doing exactly what you should be doing and following faithfully in the steps of Jesus who went before you.

Suppose ye that I am come to give peace on earth? I tell you, Nay; but rather division.

LUKE 12:51

Day 108

JOSHUA 10:1–11:15
LUKE 13:1–21
PSALM 71:1–6

Where is your hope found? In your job? Family? Financial security? Social status? In today's psalm, the author wrote that his hope is grounded firmly in his Lord. Hope and trust in God, and you won't be disappointed. This certainly doesn't mean that hoping in God is a way to avoid hardships and struggles. Instead, God will prove His trustworthiness through those times so that you can learn to hope in Him all the more.

For thou art my hope, O Lord GOD:
thou art my trust from my youth.
PSALM 71:5

The resilience of those who truly know God is remarkable. We see examples of this all through the Bible in God's prophets, disciples, apostles, and followers. In today's passage we see it in David.

Day 109

JOSHUA 11:16–13:33
LUKE 13:22–35
PSALM 71:7–16

In this psalm, his life situation does not sound like anything to be happy about—even his enemies thought that God had forsaken him. And yet, he continued to hope in God, praise Him, and speak of His righteousness. Only the Lord can grant this kind of strength and perseverance in His children.

But I will hope continually, and will yet praise thee more and more.
PSALM 71:14

Day 110

Joshua 14–16

Luke 14:1–15

Psalm 71:17–21

*A*t times God may bring you through hard trials and "sore troubles." But you can be as confident as David was in this psalm that God will raise you up again from the depths of despair. David used beautiful imagery of God comforting him on every side—His comfort surrounds and protects His people. Even in (and often *especially* in) the darkest moments, you can feel His comfort and strength sustaining you.

Thou, which hast shewed me great and sore troubles, shalt quicken me again, and shalt bring me up again from the depths of the earth. Thou shalt increase my greatness, and comfort me on every side.

Psalm 71:20–21

Would you qualify to be one of Jesus' disciples? It's a sobering question. Jesus said that only those who forsake everything they have can be His disciples. While God is not asking you to all of a sudden give away everything you have, would you be willing to if He did ask? What if your earthly comforts and treasures were taken away? How would you react? If your faith in Jesus is not dependent on earthly possessions and relationships, then you are worthy of being His disciple. Seek to know Him better so that you will have this kind of faith.

Day 111

JOSHUA 17:1–19:16
LUKE 14:16–35
PSALM 71:22–24

So likewise, whosoever he be of you
that forsaketh not all that he hath,
he cannot be my disciple.
LUKE 14:33

Day 112

JOSHUA 19:17–21:42
LUKE 15:1–10
PSALM 72:1–11

When someone comes to know the Lord, it is no small thing in heaven. In fact, Jesus declared that the angels rejoice when someone prays to receive Christ. What a marvelous thing that heaven rejoiced when you were adopted into God's family. You are a valuable part of His kingdom, worth being celebrated.

Likewise, I say unto you, there is joy in the presence of the angels of God over one sinner that repenteth.

LUKE 15:10

*A*ll of God's promises will come to pass. No good gift from Him will fail. God does not promise us things to manipulate, control, or distract. He promises us good things because He loves us in a way that we can't even comprehend. It is an entirely selfless, self-sacrificing love, the kind that we cannot fully know on earth apart from Him. So cling to His promises as truth, and look forward to their fulfillment. Just as He was faithful to the Israelites, He will be faithful to you.

Day 113

JOSHUA 21:43–22:34
LUKE 15:11–32
PSALM 72:12–20

There failed not ought of any good thing which the LORD had spoken unto the house of Israel; all came to pass.
JOSHUA 21:45

Day 114

Joshua 23–24
Luke 16:1–18
Psalm 73:1–9

It's easy to compartmentalize our lives into tidy little boxes that separate the spiritual from the everyday and earthly. Today's passage in Luke is an excellent reminder that we need to be faithful in every aspect of our lives, whether or not it seems to directly relate to the kingdom. Honor God in the way you treat your family, perform at your job or school, do your finances, etc. Be faithful in these things so that you can be entrusted with far more precious riches.

If therefore ye have not been faithful in the unrighteous mammon, who will commit to your trust the true riches?

LUKE 16:11

The first part of Psalm 73 is an anxiety-ridden, somewhat cynical view of the world. David was so overcome with the undeserved prosperity of the wicked that he began to doubt whether following a righteous path was worthwhile. He became so worked up that his thoughts were too painful to even consider. But the turning point of the psalm comes in verse 17—"Until I went into the sanctuary of God. . . " When you are anxious and overwhelmed, run to God's sanctuary. Don't neglect your time with His people, and savor the times in His courts in your own personal devotions. Being in God's presence fixes cynical perspectives and soothes anxiety.

Until I went into the sanctuary of God;
then understood I their end.
PSALM 73:17

Day 116

JUDGES 3–4
LUKE 17:11–37
PSALM 73:21–28

Why did the one former leper return? He returned because he knew where he had been and he knew that God was solely responsible for his present state. Are we as aware of who we are without God's grace? If we were, we would probably be as grateful as the man in today's passage. We too would fall at His feet so overcome with what God has done in our lives.

And one of them, when he saw that
he was healed, turned back, and with
a loud voice glorified God, and fell
down on his face at his feet, giving him
thanks: and he was a Samaritan.

LUKE 17:15–16

The publican in today's passage had the right perspective on who he was and who God is. His unworthiness to stand in the presence of a perfectly holy God was painfully apparent to him. All

he could do was humbly beg for God's mercy. In our culture that praises the bold, unhindered, and self-sufficient, the publican's behavior may seem weak. But actually, it is through this kind of weakness that we become more powerful than we can imagine. For when we empty ourselves before God, He fills us up fully with His own strength.

And the publican, standing afar off, would not lift up so much as his eyes unto heaven, but smote upon his breast, saying, God be merciful to me a sinner.
LUKE 18:13

Day 118

Judges 6:25–7:25
Luke 18:18–43
Psalm 74:4–11

God knows our natures so well. He was fully aware that He had to make Gideon's army absurdly small and weak in order for them to understand that the victory was only from God. How often do we take credit for all our successes in life? When things are going well, we pat ourselves on the back for a job well done. It's often because of our assumed self-sufficiency that God will bring challenges into our lives that force us to realize that we are sustained through Him and Him alone.

And the Lord said unto Gideon, The people that are with thee are too many for me to give the Midianites into their hands, lest Israel vaunt themselves against me, saying, Mine own hand hath saved me.

Judges 7:2

$\mathcal{Z}$acchaeus could attest to the fact that encounters with Christ change people. Zacchaeus was a selfish criminal who stole from those he levied taxes on. In the course of his career he would

have hurt many families for his own comfort and leisure. But his heart and lifestyle changed when Christ sought him out and came to his house. Don't ever imagine that such a self-absorbed and cruel sinner is past the saving power of Jesus. Christ came to earth to seek out the lost. He continues on that mission today.

And Zacchaeus stood, and said unto the Lord: Behold, Lord, the half of my goods I give to the poor; and if I have taken any thing from any man by false accusation, I restore him fourfold.

LUKE 19:8

Day 120

Judges 9:24–10:18
Luke 19:29–48
Psalm 74:18–23

The Gospel writers recorded this story of finding a donkey right where Christ had told them it would be. It may seem like an insignificant little tidbit to include in the stories of when God walked on earth. But it records a valuable story of how God ordains every detail of our lives. Even the minute details of your life matter to your God.

*And they that were sent went their way,
and found even as he had said unto them.*

Luke 19:32

*G*od is ultimately the One who promotes or demotes. Therefore, work and live as for the Lord. When your job, homework, or housework seems insignificant or thankless, remember that it is God for whom you work. He's the one who sees your efforts. He will reward you. So continue to labor hard for Him.

For promotion cometh neither from the east,
nor from the west, nor from the south.
But God is the judge: he putteth down
one, and setteth up another.
PSALM 75:6–7

Day 122

JUDGES 12:8–14:20
LUKE 20:27–47
PSALM 75:8–10

It's a probing question that should be asked: What are your motives for doing good? Do your good works stem from a desire to be praised or a desire for God to be praised? While God can certainly use deeds done for the wrong motives to His glory, you will be abundantly more blessed when your work comes from a humble desire to faithfully and fully serve your God.

Beware of the scribes, which desire to walk in long robes, and love greetings in the markets, and the highest seats in the synagogues, and the chief rooms at feasts.

LUKE 20:46

*H*ave you ever put kingdom work on hold because you felt like you didn't have enough to offer? Today's story in Luke completely negates that excuse. The poor widow in this passage gave an offering

that by the world's standards was worthless. But by God's standards it was the most valuable offering that she could have given. Fortunately, God's kingdom does not function on the same economy as our worldly kingdoms. So bring your offerings of time, talents, and treasure to Him no matter how insignificant they may seem to you.

And he said, Of a truth I say unto you, that this poor widow hath cast in more than they all: for all these have of their abundance cast in unto the offerings of God: but she of her penury hath cast in all the living that she had.
LUKE 21:3–4

Day 124

Judges 17–18
Luke 21:20–22:6
Psalm 76:8–12

This world is entirely transitory, unpredictable, and mortal. You may have painfully experienced firsthand how often things in this life change and how quickly lives, relationships, and status can be extinguished. Life can feel very much like an unmoored sailboat in a vast, choppy ocean. But in God you have the firmest foundation possible. He anchors you securely to Himself and to His plans for you. Even if this entire world were to pass away and slip into oblivion, His Word will remain steadfast. And in His Word we have hope for eternal life that is not affected by the fate of this earth.

Heaven and earth shall pass away:
but my words shall not pass away.
Luke 21:33

We have all (including today's psalmist) been in situations that cause us to question the very goodness and sovereignty of God. But instead of being spiritually near-sighted and writing God off when the here and now isn't going the way you deem it should be, expand your vision to remember His wonders of old. Call to mind the way He has cared for and sustained you (and centuries of His children) in the past. It is likely that the very struggle you're enduring now will later become one that you will look back on to recall God's faithfulness.

Hath God forgotten to be gracious? hath he in anger shut up his tender mercies? Selah. . . .
I will remember the works of the LORD:
surely I will remember thy wonders of old.
PSALM 77:9, 11

Day 126

JUDGES 20:24–21:25
LUKE 22:31–54
PSALM 77:12–20

"Not my will, but thine, be done." This is a remarkably difficult attitude to have even in minor everyday struggles. We have no problem abiding with God's will when it lines up perfectly with ours. As soon as God's plan veers away from the course that we've set for our lives, we often begin to doubt that He's really got it right after all. It's only through the power of Christ that we can superhumanly bend our will and desire to rest in God's perfect plan for us.

Saying, Father, if thou be willing,
remove this cup from me:
nevertheless not my will,
but thine, be done.

LUKE 22:42

Do we deny God in our daily lives? Maybe without even consciously realizing it? Maybe a better question is, Do we feel the kind of remorse that Peter felt over denying our Lord? Our God

is so merciful that even when we fail Him time and time again, He will forgive us and not alter His love for us. The frightened, overwhelmed Peter became so courageous in his proclamation of Christ that he was willing even to die for the cause of His Savior. You are never too weak to be out of God's love or plans.

And Peter said, Man, I know not what thou sayest. And immediately, while he yet spake, the cock crew. And the Lord turned, and looked upon Peter. And Peter remembered the word of the Lord, how he had said unto him, Before the cock crow, thou shalt deny me thrice.

LUKE 22:60–61

Day 128

Ruth 3–4
Luke 23:26–24:12
Psalm 78:5–8

Ruth beautifully embodied God's pursuit of those outside the nation of Israel and foreshadowed the time when all nations would be included in God's people. Here was this foreigner from a pagan land who ended up as an ancestor of David and, therefore, an ancestor of Christ. The glorious story of God's redemption of people from every tribe and nation was already being threaded into the genealogy of His Son. If you look back at the genealogy of Christ in Matthew 1, you'll notice that only a generation or so before Ruth, Rahab (the harlot from Jericho) was also grafted into the line of Christ. One can only wonder if Ruth and Rahab may have known each other as foreigners brought into the fold of God's people.

---

*And the women her neighbours gave it a
name, saying, There is a son born to Naomi;
and they called his name Obed: he is the
father of Jesse, the father of David.*

RUTH 4:17

H annah had an astonishingly selfless understanding of how Samuel was completely a gift from God. She had begged for a child and promised that if God granted her wish, she would give Samuel to serve in the temple of God his whole life. This is remarkable. We often grip so tightly to what God has given us freely that we forget where it came from in the first place. But Hannah was so grateful to God that she humbly loosened her grip on this good gift to return her son to the Lord.

But Hannah went not up; for she said unto her husband, I will not go up until the child be weaned, and then I will bring him, that he may appear before the Lord, and there abide for ever.

1 Samuel 1:22

Day 130

1 SAMUEL 2:22–4:22
JOHN 1:1–28
PSALM 78:17–24

*I*n the Greek philosophy of the day, the word *Logos* (translated as "Word") carried the connotation of the reason for life. So John very boldly proclaims that the Word, the reason for life, became flesh and dwelled among us. The reason for life is not a philosophy, a job, or a goal that must be attained with effort. Instead, the Logos is a Man. Life finds its deepest fulfillment in relationship with Him. He dwelled with John and now dwells in you.

In the beginning was the Word, and the Word was with God, and the Word was God. . . . And the Word was made flesh, and dwelt among us, (and we beheld his glory, the glory as of the only begotten of the Father,) full of grace and truth.

JOHN 1:1, 14

The story at the start of 1 Samuel 5 is almost comical as time and time again the city's idol is found on its face in front of the ark of God. But what is not comical at all is the truth demonstrated in this story: No other god is a match for our God. No idol that we may cling to today can stand up to the power of God. All will come crashing down at His feet. Stop holding on to things that can't possibly replace God.

And when they arose early on the morrow morning, behold, Dagon was fallen upon his face to the ground before the ark of the Lord; and the head of Dagon and both the palms of his hands were cut off upon the threshold; only the stump of Dagon was left to him.

1 Samuel 5:4

Day 132

1 Samuel 8:1–9:26
John 2
Psalm 78:34–41

In 1 Samuel 9:21, Saul tried to counter what Samuel was telling him by explaining to Samuel that he was from the smallest tribe and most insignificant family in Israel. He argued that because of this God couldn't possibly mean to anoint him king. Clearly, God must have made a mistake. Little did Saul know that choosing the most unlikely is God's usual strategy. Time and again, God uses the weak, the small, or the inhibited to do His work. Since power comes solely from Him, He does not need to choose the strong, powerful, or influential to accomplish His will.

And Saul answered and said, Am not I a Benjamite, of the smallest of the tribes of Israel? and my family the least of all the families of the tribe of Benjamin? wherefore then speakest thou so to me?

1 Samuel 9:21

Don't be surprised if you encounter opposition for the sake of Christ. Sadly, too many in this world love the darkness more than the life-giving Light. It is tragic that someone would prefer to stumble in the darkness than walk in the brilliant light of God. It is your job to shine that light of God into the darkest corners of the world so that because of you others (even if just a few) may learn to bask in the light of the Son.

1 SAMUEL 9:27–11:15
JOHN 3:1–22
PSALM 78:42–55

And this is the condemnation, that light is come into the world, and men loved darkness rather than light, because their deeds were evil. For every one that doeth evil hateth the light, neither cometh to the light, lest his deeds should be reproved.

JOHN 3:19–20

Day 134

1 Samuel 12–13
John 3:23–4:10
Psalm 78:56–66

How could a loving God give His people over to nations that hate them? God is a jealous God. He so desires us to follow Him that He will go to great lengths to make that happen. This is an incredibly good thing for us. Ease and prosperity have a way of making us forget God. Sometimes He has to remind us that our true life source can only be found in Him. And sometimes He must use hard circumstances to actually get through to us. It is, in fact, a sure sign of His love when He rebukes His people. For Him to not care and to allow you to fill your existence with deadening activities devoid of Him would be far, far worse than any trial He will lead you through.

He gave his people over also unto the sword;
and was wroth with his inheritance.

Psalm 78:62

*F*ood is essential to life. Without it we die. In John 4:34, Christ declared that His food was to do the will of His Father. Fulfilling God's will for His life was His very sustenance. Is doing

God's will as important to you as your daily food? You would notice if you went a day without food. Would you notice if you went a day without seeking God? Don't starve yourself of the necessary spiritual nourishment of seeking after God and doing His will.

Jesus saith unto them, My meat is to do the will of him that sent me, and to finish his work.
JOHN 4:34

Day 136

1 Samuel 15–16
John 4:39–54
Psalm 79:1–7

Our human perspectives and mind-sets so often blind us to an eternal and God-given perspective. We see examples of this in today's passage. The fear of the opinion of his fellow man was more powerful to Saul than his fear of God. Samuel looked at the impressive outward appearance of David's brothers and had to be reminded by God that his earthly perspective was limited. Ask God for an eternal perspective. It will certainly change the way you see things.

And it came to pass, when they were come, that he looked on Eliab, and said, Surely the Lord's anointed is before him. But the Lord said unto Samuel, Look not on his countenance, or on the height of his stature; because I have refused him: for the Lord seeth not as man seeth; for man looketh on the outward appearance, but the Lord looketh on the heart.

1 Samuel 16:6–7

David faced a terrifying enemy with the added pressure of the welfare of his entire nation resting on him. He stood up to Goliath with a courage that can only stem from a true and full knowledge

of God's power and love for His people. David knew without a shadow of a doubt that God had a plan for His people and that He would deliver the Philistines into his hand that day. It's much easier to be brave when you know going in that the battle ends in your favor. Through Christ, we too can be confident that the war ends in our favor with complete victory over death and sin. Face the world armed with the name of the Lord of hosts.

Then said David to the Philistine, Thou comest to me with a sword, and with a spear, and with a shield: but I come to thee in the name of the Lord of hosts, the God of the armies of Israel, whom thou hast defied.

1 Samuel 17:45

Day 138

1 Samuel 18–19
John 5:25–47
Psalm 80:1–7

One of the most magnificent sights in nature is when, after a storm, the clouds break to let rays of sunshine through. It's almost as if the very light of heaven has broken through the dark clouds. The language of God's face shining upon His people calls to mind a similar image. Even in the most violent of tempests, God's face is turned toward you, and His everlasting light breaks through the clouds.

Turn us again, O God of hosts, and cause thy face to shine; and we shall be saved.

PSALM 80:7

In this passage in John, Jesus asked Philip a question. But He didn't ask it in order to learn the answer. In fact, John tells us that Jesus already knew what He was going to do. When God asks you to walk through a difficult situation, or places questions in front of you that are difficult and painful to answer, take comfort in the fact that He already knows what He is going to do. Stand firmly rooted with faith in His sovereignty.

When Jesus then lifted up his eyes, and saw a great company come unto him, he saith unto Philip, Whence shall we buy bread, that these may eat? And this he said to prove him: for he himself knew what he would do.

JOHN 6:5–6

Day 140

1 Samuel 22–23

John 6:22–42

Psalm 81:1–10

It is so easy to be lulled into the trap of desiring and seeking God for what He gives rather than for who He is. Like the people in Jesus' time who sought Him because of the tangible food that they ate, we too can often seek Him for the gifts He gives. But there is so much more beauty and fulfillment to be found in seeking God to know Him. Just as Jesus went on to say, don't seek earthly bread from God but rather spiritual bread and an everlasting relationship with Him.

Jesus answered them and said, Verily, verily, I say unto you, Ye seek me, not because ye saw the miracles, but because ye did eat of the loaves, and were filled.

John 6:26

What a beautiful perspective Peter had in today's passage. Having tasted of the words of eternal life that Christ offered, he couldn't imagine ever leaving Jesus for something else. Have you been so touched by Christ as to not be able to fathom life without Him? Or is He merely a supplement to your life to be brought out on the weekends? A true relationship with Him is life changing, so strive to get to know Him more intimately.

Day 141

SAMUEL 24:1–25:31
JOHN 6:43–71
PSALM 81:11–16

Then Simon Peter answered him,
Lord, to whom shall we go?
thou hast the words of eternal life.
JOHN 6:68

Day 142

1 Samuel 25:32–27:12
John 7:1–24
Psalm 82

David had learned to let God work His perfect plan instead of assuming that God's plan lined up completely with his plan. It's easy for us to decide that we know God's will only because it's what we want. Beware of trying to impose your will on His; disappointment and anger are sure to follow. Rest in God's perfect timing instead of trying to accomplish His work for Him.

And David said to Abishai, Destroy him not: for who can stretch forth his hand against the Lord's anointed, and be guiltless? David said furthermore, As the Lord liveth, the Lord shall smite him; or his day shall come to die; or he shall descend into battle, and perish.

1 Samuel 26:9–10

The woman in today's passage in John must have been terrified to be dragged in front of a known expert in the Law with a crowd of men eager to see her stoned. But instead of meeting her accuser in that unofficial courtroom, she came face-to-face with her Savior. May we be more aware of and more disgusted by our own sin than anyone else's sin. But in our sin, may we always realize that in Christ we have an advocate and Savior, not an accuser.

When Jesus had lifted up himself, and saw none but the woman, he said unto her, Woman, where are those thine accusers? hath no man condemned thee?

JOHN 8:10

Day 143

1 SAMUEL 28–29
JOHN 7:25–8:11
PSALM 83

Day 144

1 Samuel 30–31
John 8:12–47
Psalm 84:1–4

Do we long for God's presence as though it were the very thing sustaining us? Do we cry out for God as the psalmist does in today's passage? It is an awe-inspiring and humbling thing to be allowed into the presence of a ruler of any nation. And yet, we are invited to come freely into the throne room of the King of kings. This is not something that should be taken for granted. But rather, we should take advantage of this invitation and daily enter into His courts.

My soul longeth, yea, even fainteth for the courts of the LORD: my heart and my flesh crieth out for the living God.

PSALM 84:2

Whether or not we acknowledge it, we live in a battle of light versus darkness. God is our sun, never allowing the darkness to overtake or overwhelm us. He is also our shield, protecting us from the arrows of the enemy in the heat of battle.

For the Lord God is a sun and shield:
the Lord will give grace and glory:
no good thing will he withhold
from them that walk uprightly.

Psalm 84:11

Day 146

2 Samuel 3–4
John 9:13–34
Psalm 85:1–7

The formerly blind man in today's passage has a wonderful, simple testimony. He knew and testified to one thing—he once was blind but now could see. Christ had changed him in a visible and tangible way. What are some things in your life that clearly point to Christ's work in you?

He answered and said, Whether he be a sinner or no, I know not: one thing I know, that, whereas I was blind, now I see.

John 9:25

The total abandon of David in today's passage is refreshing. He was so in love with his God and so thrilled that the ark was returning home that he danced with all his might before God. He wasn't worried about his reputation or how he might look in front of all the people watching. He was simply overwhelmed with the goodness of his God that he couldn't help but show it.

Day 147

2 Samuel 5:1–7:17
John 9:35–10:10
Psalm 85:8–13

And David danced before the Lord with all his might; and David was girded with a linen ephod.

2 Samuel 6:14

Day 148

2 Samuel 7:18–10:19
John 10:11–30
Psalm 86:1–10

Do you ever fear that if you were truly known, you couldn't be loved? Your Good Shepherd both knows you and loves you in ways that you can't even fathom. He knew you perfectly before you were even born and continues to know each of your inward thoughts. But in spite of this, He still loves you. This is not a surface love either. It is a love that would drive Him to lay down His life for you. You are intimately known and deeply loved by the Person that matters the very most.

I am the good shepherd, and know my sheep, and am known of mine. As the Father knoweth me, even so know I the Father: and I lay down my life for the sheep.

John 10:14–15

Sometimes God brings us through difficult circumstances for the purpose of increasing our faith. To those who knew and loved Lazarus, it probably would have felt like Jesus failed at

this point. He had healed so many, and yet He wasn't around to heal one of His friends. Little did they know that Jesus had an even bigger miracle in store. His plan was not merely to heal Lazarus but to raise him from the dead. When we feel as though God has missed an opportunity in our lives, we need to remember that His plan is perfect and He may just be preparing for something bigger than we could have imagined.

And I am glad for your sakes that I was not there, to the intent ye may believe; nevertheless let us go unto him.

JOHN 11:15

Day 150

2 Sam. 12:26–13:39
John 11:17–54
Psalm 87

Jesus groaned as He came to the grave where Lazarus was laid—a grave with a stone rolled over it, similar to the grave that He would be laid in shortly. He was deeply sorrowed over the death that He would soon conquer. Lazarus's resurrection was a skirmish in the ultimate battle of life over death—the battle that Christ would soon be victorious in. Even though we know the end of our story (a glorious eternal life with Christ), it is right and good to mourn over the pain and sorrow of this world as we wait for the fulfillment of God's promises.

Jesus therefore again groaning in himself cometh to the grave. It was a cave, and a stone lay upon it.

John 11:38

The chief priests in the Jewish community plotted to kill not only Jesus but Lazarus as well. All throughout history and on into the future, people will oppose Christ and go to great lengths to disprove Him. Those who are walking testimonies of His power and love will be targeted also. But it is far better to live in His truth than to live in the fear of man.

But the chief priests consulted that they might put Lazarus also to death; because that by reason of him many of the Jews went away, and believed on Jesus.

John 12:10–11

Day 152

2 Samuel 15:13–16:23
John 12:20–43
Psalm 88:10–18

If you put too much time and effort into making your life exactly how you want it here on earth, you will certainly be disappointed. Holding on to the vision of a "perfect life" will cause you to lose that perfect life. A good life on earth can only be attained when lived out with the perspective of eternity. This perspective will radically change your priorities and the way you live your life.

He that loveth his life shall lose it; and he that hateth his life in this world shall keep it unto life eternal.

JOHN 12:25

Christ preached a very countercultural message. Here was a King who washed the feet of His followers and encouraged them to do the same. Is it any wonder that some people didn't believe that this could be the King and Conqueror that was prophesied of in the Old Testament? And yet, in all His humility, He was and is far more powerful than any earthly king and warrior could ever be. He didn't conquer the oppressive nation of Rome. Instead, He conquered death by being slaughtered as a sacrificial Lamb. This is the kind of King to follow.

If I then, your Lord and Master, have washed your feet; ye also ought to wash one another's feet. For I have given you an example, that ye should do as I have done to you.

John 13:14–15

Day 154

2 Sam. 18:19–19:39
John 13:21–38
Psalm 89:7–13

God is the only one who can control the wind and the waves of the sea. He is praised for doing so in today's psalm. How poignant it would have been to the disciples when Jesus stilled the storm while they were at sea. They would have recognized that this was truly God walking among them.

Thou rulest the raging of the sea: when the waves thereof arise, thou stillest them.

Psalm 89:9

God has been moving closer to His people all throughout history. But He couldn't possibly get any closer to His children than when He walked among them on earth, right? Christ's disciples

may have thought this, which is why He told them about the Comforter that the Father would send to them. This Comforter doesn't just walk with us; He abides in us. He has no physical restrictions regarding space or time, meaning He can be with all of God's children simultaneously and continuously. He is ever present with you and will be so forever.

And I will pray the Father,
and he shall give you another
Comforter, that he may
abide with you for ever.

JOHN 14:16

Day 156

2 Samuel 22:1–23:7
John 14:18–15:27
Psalm 89:19–29

David spoke from experience when he asserted that God was his lamp to lighten the darkness around him. His life was far from easy. He had friends and family turn against him and force him into a life of running and hiding. But through even the darkest of circumstances, God remained as a faithful light by his side to illuminate his steps and keep him safe from harm. No matter the situation, God is your lamp as well. The darker it gets, the more brilliantly His light shines.

For thou art my lamp,
O Lord: and the Lord
will lighten my darkness.
2 Samuel 22:29

God made a covenant with His servant David, and He has stood by that covenant through generations and generations. This covenant will stand forever since one of David's descendants sits on the eternal throne. God does not make His promises and covenants lightly because He will never go back on a promise He has made.

My covenant will I not break, nor alter the thing that is gone out of my lips. Once have I sworn by my holiness that I will not lie unto David. His seed shall endure for ever, and his throne as the sun before me.
Psalm 89:34–36

Day 158

1 Kings 1
John 16:23–17:5
Psalm 89:38–52

*A*s Jesus prepared to go to His death, He told His disciples that two things were certain: first, that in the world they would have trials and tribulations, but, second, that in these they would have a joyful peace because Christ had overcome the world. Don't be surprised when trials and difficulties surface in your life. Christ gave us fair warning that these would come. But in Him and in the knowledge of His victory over death, sin, and sorrow, you can have a peace that is unmatched by anything this world can offer. You can indeed face this world with good cheer.

These things I have spoken unto you, that in me ye might have peace. In the world ye shall have tribulation: but be of good cheer; I have overcome the world.

JOHN 16:33

Isn't it remarkable that in the pages of the Bible is recorded for all time a prayer that Jesus prayed for you? While the inevitability of the cross loomed in front of Him, He prayed for His current followers and all those who would come after. As a follower of Christ, He prayed for you.

Neither pray I for these alone,
but for them also which shall
believe on me through their word.
John 17:20

Day 160

1 Kings 3–4
John 18:1–27
Psalm 90:13–17

Wouldn't our prayers be so much more productive if we stopped praying for a situation to turn out specifically how we wanted it to and instead prayed for wisdom and discernment? We must humbly realize that God's plan, whatever that may be, is so much better than our plan. So ask Him for wisdom and patience to discern His will.

Give therefore thy servant an understanding heart to judge thy people, that I may discern between good and bad: for who is able to judge this thy so great a people?

1 Kings 3:9

When you are one of God's children, held in His powerful hand, you are immortal until the day that He has ordained to bring you home. Nothing can touch you outside of His perfect plan. Even with ten thousand falling at your side, you will stand strong until the day when God has decided to bestow on you the glorious privilege of being admitted into heaven.

Day 161

1 KINGS 5–6
JOHN 18:28–19:5
PSALM 91:1–10

*A thousand shall fall at thy side,
and ten thousand at thy right hand;
but it shall not come nigh thee.*

PSALM 91:7

Day 162

1 KINGS 7
JOHN 19:6–24
PSALM 91:11–16

The irony and stubborn truth displayed in what Pilate wrote for the cross of Christ is really very beautiful. Even during His humiliating death, it was being proclaimed to all who passed by that Jesus was King. The Gospel can never be silenced, not even by an angry mob who killed the very Son of God.

This title then read many of the Jews: for the place where Jesus was crucified was nigh to the city: and it was written in Hebrew, and Greek, and Latin. Then said the chief priests of the Jews to Pilate, Write not, The King of the Jews; but that he said, I am King of the Jews. Pilate answered, What I have written I have written.

JOHN 19:20–22

*I*magine how awe inspiring it must have been to see the cloud of God's presence fill the holy place. How remarkable it would have been to be one of the people standing there, seeing the very presence of

God and knowing that He dwelled with you. And yet, you have a greater gift than that. While the people were unable to enter the holy place, you can go right up to the very throne of God. The curtain that was torn in two at Christ's death will never be sewn together again. You have eternal access to your heavenly Father. His Spirit dwells in and with you.

And it came to pass, when the priests were come out of the holy place, that the cloud filled the house of the Lord.

1 Kings 8:10

Day 164

1 Kings 8:54–10:13
John 20:1–18
Psalm 92:10–15

Those who walk with Christ will still be fruitful even in their old age. Far from being forgotten members of society, the older generation has so much to offer about their long and faithful walk with Christ. As an elderly person, don't be afraid to share your testimony of God's faithfulness. As a younger person, seek out those from whom you can gain wisdom and the life perspective of a long life well lived.

They shall still bring forth fruit in old age;
they shall be fat and flourishing.

Psalm 92:14

There is not enough room in the Gospel accounts to tell the stories of all the people whose lives were radically changed by Christ. But the accounts of the real Man who touched and changed real

people are there so that we too, generations later, can believe in Him. Write down your own accounts of how Christ changes and shapes your life. Remembering His faithfulness will strengthen your faith and give you abundant life through His name.

But these are written, that ye might believe that Jesus is the Christ, the Son of God; and that believing ye might have life through his name.
JOHN 20:31

Day 166

1 Kings 12:1–13:10
John 21
Psalm 94:1–11

Rehoboam very unwisely followed the counsel of his foolish friends rather than the counsel of the wise men who had far more experience with ruling people. Who are your counselors? Who are you surrounding yourself with whose thoughts and attitudes are rubbing off on you? Choose your friends and counselors wisely since those who are closest to you have a powerful say in your life.

But he forsook the counsel of the old men, which they had given him, and consulted with the young men that were grown up with him, and which stood before him.

1 Kings 12:8

W e rarely think that discipline and chastening are blessings. But when God teaches and rebukes you through His Word or through others in your life, you ought to be grateful. He is graciously pulling

you back from a dangerous ledge and sparing you from a long fall. Sometimes God's discipline may seem harsher than at other times, but each correction ultimately brings you healing and guides you into a closer walk with God.

Day 167

1 Kings 13:11–14:31
Acts 1:1–11
Psalm 94:12–23

Blessed is the man whom thou chastenest,
O Lord, and teachest him out of thy law.
Psalm 94:12

Day 168

1 Kings 15:1–16:20
Acts 1:12–26
Psalm 95

God does not abandon His plan. He covenanted with David that one of his descendants would always reign. Even with all the evil kings that reigned after David, He did not disregard His promise. And now Jesus, a descendant of David, will reign forever. Remember that you serve a God who keeps His promises and doesn't change His mind. Therefore, you can have a sure confidence that no matter what is happening in your life right now, it is definitely part of God's perfect plan.

Nevertheless for David's sake did the LORD his God give him a lamp in Jerusalem, to set up his son after him, and to establish Jerusalem.

1 Kings 15:4

The psalmist desires all the earth to sing to the Lord. Generations later at Pentecost, this vision of the psalmist started to become a reality. The Holy Spirit descended, allowing people from many nations to hear the Gospel in their own language. The good news continued to spread from there into all the earth. One day people from every nation will be singing God's praise together in the throne room of their Savior.

O sing unto the LORD a new song:
sing unto the LORD, all the earth.
PSALM 96:1

Day 170

1 KINGS 18:20–19:21
ACTS 2:22–41
PSALM 96:9–13

*E*lijah taunted and ridiculed the prophets of Baal, who were enemies of God. When it came time for him to show Israel who the true God was, his prayer was a beautiful picture of someone who walked humbly with God and had a personal relationship with Him. He asked that God would consume the sacrifice, not so he would look good but so the people would know who their God was. God answered the faithful prayer of His servant and shattered any disbelief in the crowd by sending down fire from heaven.

Elijah the prophet came near, and said, LORD God of Abraham, Isaac, and of Israel, let it be known this day that thou art God in Israel, and that I am thy servant, and that I have done all these things at thy word. Hear me, O LORD, hear me, that this people may know that thou art the LORD God, and that thou hast turned their heart back again. Then the fire of the LORD fell, and consumed the burnt sacrifice.

1 KINGS 18:36–38

The transformation of the lame man in Acts is a testament to God's ability to completely transform a person. Not only did He fix what was wrong in the man's legs, but He also created muscle strength and coordination that the man would never have had due to his disability—no physical therapy and long rehabilitation necessary. Even with all the incredible medical and scientific advancements we have been blessed to make, we can never match the power of the Creator to restore His broken creation. That is a God who truly deserves to be praised.

And he leaping up stood, and walked, and entered with them into the temple, walking, and leaping, and praising God.

Acts 3:8

Day 172

1 Kings 21:1–22:28
Acts 4:1–22
Psalm 97:7–12

*I*t's easy to become overwhelmed by the evil in this world and to loathe its very existence. While we have to live in this imperfect world until Christ brings us home or comes again, take heart that this hatred of evil is a sure sign that you love God. When you have aligned yourself with someone, you end up loving or hating the things that person loves or hates. God hates evil even more than you, and as your heart becomes more like His, you will see things even more vividly from His perspective. Ask Him to continue to mold your heart to be like His.

Ye that love the Lord, hate evil: he preserveth the souls of his saints; he delivereth them out of the hand of the wicked.

Psalm 97:10

*I*njustice is rampant on this earth. But God judges with righteousness and equity. He does not judge based on personal bias or prejudice. He does not take into account skin color, age, nationality, or gender. His judgment is pure and holy. He is coming to judge the earth in a way that will finally bring true justice to the wicked and peace and reconciliation to the oppressed.

Day 173

1 Kin. 22:29–2 Kin. 1
Acts 4:23–5:11
Psalm 98

[The Lord] cometh to judge the earth:
with righteousness shall he judge the
world, and the people with equity.
Psalm 98:9

Day 174

2 Kings 2–3
Acts 5:12–28
Psalm 99

The apostles were accused of filling an entire city with their doctrine. Their relentless preaching of the Gospel was so pervasive that the officials of the city took note and felt like something had to be done to address the rapid spread of their teachings. Wouldn't it be amazing if we could fill the cities we live in with this same life-giving doctrine? To be accused of the same thing as these faithful and courageous apostles would truly be an honor.

Saying, Did not we straitly command you that ye should not teach in this name? and, behold, ye have filled Jerusalem with your doctrine, and intend to bring this man's blood upon us.

Acts 5:28

Could Elisha, through God's power, have solved all the widow's problems in today's passage without having her do anything? Of course he could have. But, instead, we're presented with

a valuable model of helping those in need. The woman first worked to get empty vessels from all her neighbors, and then God performed the miracle. As God knew and demonstrated, it is often very constructive to allow the person in need to be part of the solution and not just a bystanding recipient of it.

Then he said, Go, borrow thee vessels abroad of all thy neighbours, even empty vessels; borrow not a few. And when thou art come in, thou shalt shut the door upon thee and upon thy sons, and shalt pour out into all those vessels, and thou shalt set aside that which is full.

2 Kings 4:3–4

Day 176

2 KINGS 5:1–6:23
ACTS 7:1–16
PSALM 101

Oh, that God would open our eyes as He did the eyes of Elisha's servant that we too might see the mighty army arrayed to protect us and to carry out God's will. We are never in this battle alone. How much more courageously would you step into battle if you were aware that you are always surrounded by a victorious, heavenly army?

And he answered, Fear not: for they that be with us are more than they that be with them. And Elisha prayed, and said, LORD, I pray thee, open his eyes, that he may see. And the LORD opened the eyes of the young man; and he saw: and, behold, the mountain was full of horses and chariots of fire round about Elisha.

2 KINGS 6:16–17

G od does not just save those who are already perfect and have their act together. In fact, the three men who wrote the most books of the Bible are all murderers—Moses (as we read about in today's passage), David (killed Uriah), and Paul (looked on in approval as Stephen was murdered). These three pillars of the faith were far from perfect men. And yet, God used them to carry out His flawless plan. If He could use them, He can certainly use you as well.

And seeing one of them suffer wrong, he defended him, and avenged him that was oppressed, and smote the Egyptian.
ACTS 7:24

Day 178

2 Kings 8:16–9:37
Acts 7:37–53
Psalm 102:8–17

The psalmist in today's passage understood his own frailty. He knew that his life was like a flickering shadow and grass that withers rapidly. But he had faith in something greater than himself. While his life was merely a vapor, his God endures forever. While most of us are forgotten soon after we depart this earth, our God will be remembered and praised throughout all eternity. Put your effort into glorifying and magnifying Him during this life rather than magnifying yourself.

My days are like a shadow that declineth;
and I am withered like grass. But thou,
O Lord, shall endure for ever; and thy
remembrance unto all generations.

Psalm 102:11–12

The people who led the persecution of the early Church must have felt like they were doing a good job of squelching the Gospel of Christ. After all, those who adhered to the teachings of Christ as the Messiah were scattering under the persecution. But God's plan and the inevitable advancement of the Gospel cannot be stopped so easily. In fact, God used the very persecution of His people to more quickly reach others for Christ. Had persecution not forced the Christians away from their homes, it would have taken longer for the good news to spread around the world.

Day 179

2 Kings 10–11
Acts 7:54–8:8
Psalm 102:18–28

Therefore they that were scattered abroad
went every where preaching the word.
Acts 8:4

Day 180

2 KINGS 12–13
ACTS 8:9–40
PSALM 103:1–9

*G*od has lovingly planned the steps of His children even down to the smallest details. The eunuch that Philip witnessed to in today's passage was reading in Isaiah 53. He came to embrace Christ that very day. We can only assume that this new believer would have kept reading in Isaiah. A few chapters later in Isaiah 56 he would have come across an exquisite passage specifically talking about the family that a eunuch has as a follower of God. How beautiful that God not only brought Philip to explain the Gospel to him, but that God also showed him through His Word that he was loved and had a place in God's family.

And Philip said, If thou believest with all thine heart, thou mayest. And he answered and said, I believe that Jesus Christ is the Son of God.

ACTS 8:37

God knows that you are frail. He knows that you are prone to certain weaknesses and sins. He remembers that you were born in sin and must often fight your very sin nature to serve Him. You serve a God who, in His holiness, demands perfection—but who, in His love, has granted you that perfection based on no effort of your own. Don't let guilt or insecurities over your shortcomings have any place in your service to God.

Day 181

2 Kings 14–15
Acts 9:1–16
Psalm 103:10–14

For he knoweth our frame;
he remembereth that we are dust.

Psalm 103:14

Day 182

2 Kings 16–17
Acts 9:17–31
Psalm 103:15–22

God will build His Church. Sometimes He builds it through the miraculous conversion of enemies of the Gospel—people like Saul. But more often He builds it through the faithful, humble, and relentless service of His children—people like Barnabas and Ananias. Whether your conversion was an elaborate "Damascus road" experience or a simple acceptance of Christ at a young age, it was a miracle that day when God ushered you into the kingdom of His Son. He can and will use every sinner who has been saved by grace.

But Barnabas took him, and brought him to the apostles, and declared unto them how he had seen the Lord in the way, and that he had spoken to him, and how he had preached boldly at Damascus in the name of Jesus.

Acts 9:27

$\mathcal{P}$eter—a miracle-working, mighty, and faithful servant of God—was called to Joppa because another mighty, faithful servant of God had died. This servant, Dorcas, had not restored sight to the blind or raised anyone from the dead, but her work was so significant that a group of people implored Peter to bring her back to life. And God chose to grant their supplication. God can work through miracles, but He can also work through a faithful daughter of His who made garments for those in need.

Day 183

2 Kings 18:1–19:7
Acts 9:32–10:16
Psalm 104:1–9

Then Peter arose and went with them. When he was come, they brought him into the upper chamber: and all the widows stood by him weeping, and shewing the coats and garments which Dorcas made, while she was with them.

Acts 9:39

Day 184

2 KINGS 19:8–20:21
ACTS 10:17–33
PSALM 104:10–23

Fear is a powerful weapon. The Assyrians understood this as they attempted to destroy the morale of God's people with terrifying taunts. But fear is no match for God. Hezekiah did what we all should do—when confronted with a seemingly indestructible enemy, Hezekiah laid the whole situation before God. He didn't try to figure it out on his own. Rather, he went to the One who was mightier than he or the Assyrians or fear itself.

And Hezekiah received the letter of the hand of the messengers, and read it: and Hezekiah went up into the house of the LORD, and spread it before the LORD.

2 KINGS 19:14

*C*ornelius sent men to go visit Peter. This seems like a fairly simple story in the book of Acts. But, it is a glorious step for God's kingdom as it is the official inclusion of the Gentiles into the Gospel of Christ. God made it clear to Peter that there was no longer any national distinction of God's people. People from all nations and languages were made clean and granted the blessing to be adopted as God's children.

Day 185

2 KINGS 21:1—22:20
ACTS 10:34—11:18
PSALM 104: 24—30

Now while Peter doubted in himself what this vision which he had seen should mean, behold, the men which were sent from Cornelius had made enquiry for Simon's house, and stood before the gate, and called, and asked whether Simon, which was surnamed Peter, were lodged there.

ACTS 10:17—18

Day 186

2 Kings 23
Acts 11:19–12:17
Psalm 104:31–35

Josiah understood who he was and who God was. The title and position of king did not make him think that he was equal to his heavenly King. He understood that all understanding and guidance comes from the Lord. Therefore, he turned to God with all his heart, soul, and might. Have you done the same?

And like unto him was there no king before him, that turned to the Lord with all his heart, and with all his soul, and with all his might, according to all the law of Moses; neither after him arose there any like him.

2 Kings 23:25

Though your relationship with God is deeply personal, it should not be totally private. You should openly give thanks to God and declare to others what He has done for you. If you truly grasped the depth of His grace to you, you would not be able to contain His praise or keep your love of Him from others. So sing unto Him and talk of His wondrous works.

O give thanks unto the LORD; call upon his name: make known his deeds among the people. Sing unto him, sing psalms unto him: talk ye of all his wondrous works.

PSALM 105:1–2

Day 188

1 Chronicles 1–2
Acts 13:14–43
Psalm 105:8–15

When God made His covenant with Abraham and promised him that his descendants would be as numerous as the stars, Abraham probably never could have imagined how immensely God would fulfill that promise. God has remembered His covenant and brought to Himself innumerable spiritual descendants of Abraham from all over the earth. Because of your faith in God, you are a direct fulfillment of God's promise.

He hath remembered his covenant for ever,
the word which he commanded to a thousand
generations. . . . When they were but a few men
in number; yea, very few, and strangers in it.

PSALM 105:8, 12

In 1 Chronicles 4:10, we read about Jabez, whose prayer for blessing, prosperity, and protection was granted. We can imagine that he would have lived a happy and joyful life. And yet, in Acts we read about followers of Christ who were being persecuted, beaten, and imprisoned. But even in these circumstances they were filled with joy. When it comes to living a joy-filled life, the circumstances don't matter. Whom you serve does.

And the disciples were filled with joy,
and with the Holy Ghost.
Acts 13:52

Day 190

Having been declared gods by the local people, it would have been easy for Paul and Barnabas to see this as their free ticket out of persecution and let the people continue to treat them as gods. But they did not deny their God to take the easy way out. Instead, they declared themselves as mere men. God could (and sometimes does) send impressive angels to declare His Word, but He most often uses flawed and weak humans. Through these broken vessels He can shine the light of His power more clearly.

And saying, Sirs, why do ye these things? We also are men of like passions with you, and preach unto you that ye should turn from these vanities unto the living God, which made heaven, and earth, and the sea, and all things that are therein.

Acts 14:15

God miraculously sustained the Israelites through the wilderness and brought them into a rich promised land. He did this so that they might serve and obey Him. But instead, the people more often disobeyed and disappointed Him. God has also brought you into the promised land of His kingdom. Don't make the same mistake as the Israelites who took His blessings and provision for granted. Thank God and serve Him for all He has done for you.

Day 191

1 Chron. 7:1–9:9
Acts 15:1–18
Psalm 105:37–45

And gave them the lands of the heathen:
and they inherited the labour of the people;
that they might observe his statutes,
and keep his laws. Praise ye the Lord.
Psalm 105:44–45

Day 192

1 Chron. 9:10–11:9
Acts 15:19–41
Psalm 106:1–12

Today's passage in Acts 15 feels slightly uncomfortable. Two of the leading apostles who were working together to spread the Gospel had a disagreement so strong that they had to separate. This seems like a major setback in the advancement of the Gospel. But God used even this for His purposes. Instead of working side by side, Paul and Barnabas were able to reach more people by going their separate ways and spreading the Gospel to different countries and people.

And the contention was so sharp between them,
that they departed asunder one from the other:
and so Barnabas took Mark, and sailed unto Cyprus.

Acts 15:39

It seems so absurd that the Israelites would have created an idol of a common animal to replace the God whose very presence they had witnessed in the pillar of fire and cloud. But don't we often do the same thing? We trade the rich bounties that are available to us in God's Word for worthless shows or games. Or we belittle the holy and mighty God into a mere genie whom we only talk to when we want something. Strive to recognize and know the glorious God for who He really is.

Thus they changed their glory into the similitude of an ox that eateth grass.
PSALM 106:20

Day 194

The concept of Jesus may sound pretty nice, or at least nonthreatening, to most people . . .until He gets in the way of their comfort. We live in a world where comfort and prosperity are god. The Jesus that we preach may be offensive to people, as He forces them to come to terms with their sin and give up things that they have held to be precious. But the riches that are in Christ are far greater than any riches that this earth can offer. We can't dare risk not sharing such an important message because we're afraid of how it will be received.

And when her masters saw that the hope of their gains was gone, they caught Paul and Silas, and drew them into the marketplace unto the rulers.

Acts 16:19

The apostles were accused of turning the world upside down. How incredible would it be if those words were spoken again of God's people! May we so unwaveringly stand for truth in the face of opposition and unabashedly proclaim Christ as the only way to true life that we turn the world on its head.

And when they found them not, they drew Jason and certain brethren unto the rulers of the city, crying, These that have turned the world upside down are come hither also.
Acts 17:6

Day 196

1 Chronicles 18–20
Acts 17:15–34
Psalm 106:44–48

Paul knew and understood the culture in which he was preaching. In today's passage, he even quoted the society's poets. It's important to know whom you are talking to when sharing the Gospel so that you can formulate your message to be the most understandable to your culture. This can be a powerful tool as long as the fundamental message and natural power of the Gospel are not softened or changed.

For in him we live, and move, and have our being;
as certain also of your own poets have said,
For we are also his offspring.

Acts 17:28

Today's passage in 1 Chronicles is one of the few times that Satan is mentioned in the Old Testament. But even when he's not spoken of directly, you can recognize his scent as his evil work is woven throughout the narratives. It is vitally important that we remember that there is a spiritual battle raging in this world at all times. We will be ill-equipped if we don't train for such a battle. Our enemy is real; so be on your guard. But remember that our Ally is stronger and can thwart any evil plans the devil can devise.

And Satan stood up against Israel,
and provoked David to number Israel.

1 CHRONICLES 21:1

Day 198

1 Chronicles 23–25
Acts 18:24–19:10
Psalm 107:10–16

When Aquila and Priscilla heard Apollos speak, they realized that he did not have a completely full or accurate knowledge of the Gospel. In response to this, they did not spend their energy talking behind his back about how ignorant he was. Instead, they took him in and trained him in the fullness of the message of Christ. Wouldn't we spend our time so much more wisely by talking less about a problem and working more to fix it?

And he began to speak boldly in the synagogue:
whom when Aquila and Priscilla had heard,
they took him unto them, and expounded
unto him the way of God more perfectly.

ACTS 18:26

The writer of today's psalm had firsthand experience of the love and saving power of God. This personal knowledge drove him to wish that others would praise God and know of His wonderful works as well. Does God's goodness to you inspire you to tell others about Him and cause you to work hard to let others know of His wonderful works?

Then they cry unto the LORD in their trouble, and he saveth them out of their distresses. He sent his word, and healed them, and delivered them from their destructions. Oh that men would praise the LORD for his goodness, and for his wonderful works to the children of men!

PSALM 107:19–21

Day 200

1 Chronicles 28–29
Acts 19:23–41
Psalm 107:33–38

*I*n today's passage, David spoke beautifully personal words to his son Solomon, encouraging him to be strong and courageous and to rely on God. David knew that his God would continue to be faithful to the next generation. Are you passing on your faith to the next generation? It is a beautiful thing when the surpassing value of a personal relationship with God is passed down to the children's children and so on. It is the best possible inheritance.

And David said to Solomon his son, Be strong and of good courage, and do it: fear not, nor be dismayed: for the Lord God, even my God, will be with thee; he will not fail thee, nor forsake thee, until thou hast finished all the work for the service of the house of the Lord.

1 Chronicles 28:20

God does not do things as the world does. While we celebrate the rich, beautiful, and powerful, He delights in the poor, lonely, and needy. It would do us good to see the world through His eyes and to value what He values.

He poureth contempt upon princes, and causeth them to wander in the wilderness, where there is no way. Yet setteth he the poor on high from affliction, and maketh him families like a flock.

Psalm 107:40–41

Day 202

2 CHRON. 4:1–6:11
ACTS 20:17–38
PSALM 108

Paul knew that bonds and afflictions waited for him in every city where he preached. This knowledge would cause many of us to give up. And yet, Paul talks about finishing his course with joy even in the face of this persecution. The only way that he could have this kind of joyful attitude amid unavoidable suffering was because he knew his God very well. His joy was entirely disconnected from his circumstances and completely rooted in his relationship with God and his hope in an eternity with his Savior.

Save that the Holy Ghost witnesseth in every city, saying that bonds and afflictions abide me. But none of these things move me, neither count I my life dear unto myself, so that I might finish my course with joy, and the ministry, which I have received of the Lord Jesus, to testify the gospel of the grace of God.

ACTS 20:23–24

Solomon spoke rightly that not even the highest heaven can contain God. Because of this, he wondered that God could ever dwell on earth with men. And yet, He did dwell on earth, as a humble and self-sacrificing Man. And now He dwells in us. That the almighty God condescended to dwell among us and in us is a truth almost too beautiful to fathom.

2 CHRON. 6:12–7:10
ACTS 21:1–14
PSALM 109:1–20

*But will God in very deed dwell with
men on the earth? behold, heaven and the
heaven of heavens cannot contain thee;
how much less this house which I have built!*

2 CHRONICLES 6:18

Day 204

2 Chron. 7:11–9:28
Acts 21:15–32
Psalm 109:21–31

It's important to make wise decisions about when to bend to cultural norms for the sake of the Gospel. In today's passage, Paul purified himself according to Jewish custom. This was not something that he as a Christian needed to do. He did this solely for the sake of the Gospel, believing that it would allow him to reach more people for Christ.

Then Paul took the men, and the next day purifying himself with them entered into the temple, to signify the accomplishment of the days of purification, until that an offering should be offered for every one of them.

Acts 21:26

$\mathcal{R}$ehoboam did evil because he did not prepare his heart to seek the Lord. What steps have you taken to prepare your heart to seek God? Do you have a regular devotional time? Do you

faithfully attend church? Are you committed to reading and memorizing God's Word? If you have not humbled yourself to seek and serve God, nothing that you do can be righteous in His sight. Set your heart to seek God, and you will find Him. He will reward you for seeking.

And he did evil, because he prepared
not his heart to seek the LORD.
2 CHRONICLES 12:14

Day 206

2 Chronicles 13–15
Acts 22:17–23:11
Psalm 110:4–7

*A*ny battle fought against the living God is a losing battle. The battle to keep your indulgent sins is a battle where you are pitted against God, and you will lose to His holiness. The battle of death over life has already been lost by the devil because he was foolish enough to go up against his Maker. Choose sides with your Savior—you will always be on the winning side.

And, behold, God himself is with us for our captain, and his priests with sounding trumpets to cry alarm against you. O children of Israel, fight ye not against the Lord God of your fathers; for ye shall not prosper.

2 Chronicles 13:12

It may at times feel like God is not actively involved in the world or that He has given up on a creation that has strayed so far from Him. But this is not true. He is constantly watching the movement of His creation. He shows Himself as a strong defense to those whose hearts are His. God is not an inactive and disconnected observer. He is already aware of your circumstances, so call out to Him in your need.

For the eyes of the Lord run to and fro throughout the whole earth, to shew himself strong in the behalf of them whose heart is perfect toward him. Herein thou hast done foolishly: therefore from henceforth thou shalt have wars.

2 Chronicles 16:9

Day 208

2 Chronicles 18–19
Acts 24:22–25:12
Psalm 112

Micaiah was faithful in relaying messages from God and was therefore hated by the king of Israel because he never told the king what he wanted to hear. You may sometimes find yourself in the same situation where being faithful to the truth of God and His Word puts you at odds with those around you. May we have the same courage as God's faithful prophets to continue to speak His truth no matter what the reception.

And the king of Israel said unto Jehoshaphat, There is yet one man, by whom we may enquire of the Lord: but I hate him; for he never prophesied good unto me, but always evil: the same is Micaiah the son of Imla. And Jehoshaphat said, Let not the king say so.

2 Chronicles 18:7

We ought to pray remembering and relying on God's promises and faithfulness. Jehoshaphat prayed in the light of God's past work and His present promises. Because he knew his God to be a promise keeper, he was able to go into battle praising God (2 Chronicles 20:21). You can march into whatever battle you are facing praising God as well. When the outcome is already decided by the past work of Christ, there is no reason to fear. There is nothing left to do but praise.

And said, O Lord God of our fathers, art not thou God in heaven? and rulest not thou over all the kingdoms of the heathen? and in thine hand is there not power and might, so that none is able to withstand thee? Art not thou our God, who didst drive out the inhabitants of this land before thy people Israel, and gavest it to the seed of Abraham thy friend for ever?

2 Chronicles 20:6–7

Day 210

*I*t's easy to dwell on the things in your life that are not going well. But are you aware of how blessed you are solely based on your relationship with Christ? No matter what circumstance you are in, you are beyond fortunate. Paul knew how blessed he was because of his walk with God and wished that others might also know the depths of the riches that he had every day. He had a truly good life that was not affected by chains or suffering.

And Paul said, I would to God, that not only thou, but also all that hear me this day, were both almost, and altogether such as I am, except these bonds.

Acts 26:29

a good mentor is remarkably valuable. When Jehoiada was alive, Joash did what was right in God's sight. When Jehoiada died, Joash began to be influenced by far less wise people and, tragically, turned from God. Don't be afraid to reach out to mentor someone—it could be the difference between that person choosing to follow God or not. At the same time, seek out a mentor for yourself that will guide you in the way of Christ.

Now after the death of Jehoiada came the princes of Judah, and made obeisance to the king. Then the king hearkened unto them.
2 Chronicles 24:17

Day 212

2 Chron. 25:17–27:9
Acts 27:21–28:6
Psalm 115:11–18

Paul knew the plan that God had for him and recognized that he was immortal until that plan was fulfilled. His faith in God's purposes was rock solid. Not even things as lethal as a shipwreck or poisonous snake could alter the course that God had set for him.

Wherefore, sirs, be of good cheer: for I believe God,
that it shall be even as it was told me.

Acts 27:25

The "sect" of Christianity was spoken against everywhere. The adherents to this sect preached of life that was released from the bonds of the Law. They preached of salvation based on no merit of one's own. They spoke of eternal life with God in heaven secured by the sacrifice of His Son. Isn't it remarkable that there could be so much resistance to such a beautiful message?

But we desire to hear of thee what thou thinkest: for as concerning this sect, we know that every where it is spoken against.
ACTS 28:22

Day 214

2 Chron. 29:20–30:27

Romans 1:1–17

Psalm 116:6–19

For those of us who have lost loved ones who are in Christ (or for those who are facing an imminent death), keep in mind that the death of God's saints is not the end. The death of His children is precious in His sight. We do not pass from this world into the next forgotten and on our own. Rather, we are led through by our faithful guide who overcame death on our behalf. A beautiful celebration awaits us on the other side. Celebrate the lives and deaths of God's children, for our Father does.

Precious in the sight of the
Lord is the death of his saints.

Psalm 116:15

What a beautiful and inspiring speech we read from King Hezekiah in today's passage. The terrifying and brutal force of Assyria was threatening God's people. But instead of giving in to

fear, Hezekiah relied on his God. No matter how big or fearful a force is up against you, you will always have more on your side because you have a heavenly army led by the everlasting God fighting for you. Being on God's side automatically puts you in the majority.

Be strong and courageous, be not afraid nor dismayed for the king of Assyria, nor for all the multitude that is with him: for there be more with us than with him: with him is an arm of flesh; but with us is the LORD our God to help us, and to fight our battles. And the people rested themselves upon the words of Hezekiah king of Judah.

2 CHRONICLES 32:7–8

Day 216

2 CHRON. 33:1–34:7
ROMANS 2
PSALM 118:1–18

We have an innate understanding of the moral law written on our hearts that proves the existence of a higher order. No matter how hard people may fight against the idea of a Creator, their very innermost conscience speaks and witnesses of Him. An instinctual knowledge of Him is inevitable. This means that however hard some people may work to harden their hearts and minds to Christ, they are without excuse on the day when they stand before their Maker.

For when the Gentiles, which have not the law,
do by nature the things contained in the law, these,
having not the law, are a law unto themselves:
which shew the work of the law written in their
hearts, their conscience also bearing witness,
and their thoughts the mean while accusing
or else excusing one another.

ROMANS 2:14–15

When it comes to our pre-salvation standing before God, we are all on an even playing field. We have all sinned and are in desperate need of His righteous covering. In God's eyes, there is no difference regarding race, gender, socioeconomic status, physical ability, or beauty. None of us can attain to His standards on our own. If God does not cater His message based on physical, financial, or social standards, then neither should we.

Even the righteousness of God which is by faith of Jesus Christ unto all and upon all them that believe: for there is no difference: for all have sinned, and come short of the glory of God.

Romans 3:22–23

Day 218

2 Chron. 35:20–36:23
Romans 3:27–4:25
Psalm 118:24–29

"This is the day which the Lord hath made; we will rejoice and be glad in it." This is a mind-set and a decision to be made each and every morning—*God has made today; therefore I will be glad.* If at the moment your life is such that it is hard to find things to rejoice in, at least you can be glad that God has given you another new day with new opportunities and new blessings from Him. He has planned out this day for you. Rejoice in the new day that God gives you.

This is the day which the Lord hath made;
we will rejoice and be glad in it.

Psalm 118:24

Where does your peace come from? Not from relationships, physical healing, or more money. It comes from being justified before God. You know you stand clean and spotless before a holy God and that because of this you are guaranteed a life of eternity in His glory. This is true peace, to know that you have been saved by grace and that nothing can touch you outside of His will for you.

Therefore being justified by faith, we have peace with God through our Lord Jesus Christ: by whom also we have access by faith into this grace wherein we stand, and rejoice in hope of the glory of God.

ROMANS 5:1—2

Day 220

Ezra 4–5
Romans 6:1–7:6
Psalm 119:9–16

Memorize God's Word. Having God's Word in your heart and mind is remarkably powerful. It has the ability to keep you from sinning and to guide you in the will of God. When temptations arise, quote scripture to yourself and brandish the sword that God has given you in His Word. The devil will flee from a fight where the unerring Word of God is boldly used as a defense. Let God's Word reign in your heart to dethrone the sin that Christ sacrificed so much to conquer (Romans 6:12).

Thy word have I hid in mine heart,
that I might not sin against thee.

Psalm 119:11

The stories recorded in Ezra and Nehemiah are a marvelous demonstration of how God is in control no matter how out of control a situation may appear to our eyes. The people's mission to rebuild the house of God was constantly facing the threat of termination. In today's passage, King Darius (a ruler from an enemy nation that had captured God's people) not only allowed them to continue work, but he even assisted them with their project. God has never lost control. He is always sovereign.

Moreover I make a decree what ye shall do to the elders of these Jews for the building of this house of God: that of the king's goods, even of the tribute beyond the river, forthwith expenses be given unto these men, that they be not hindered.

Ezra 6:8

Day 222

EZRA 7:27–9:4
ROMANS 8:1–27
PSALM 119:33–40

There is no condemnation for you who are in Christ. Do you really grasp that? Covered by Christ's blood-washed robes, you cannot be condemned. You no longer need to live under the yoke of slavery to sin and the Law. Your freedom in Christ releases you from a life of desperately trying to reach an unattainable standard. This doesn't mean that you shouldn't strive to live a righteous life. But now that righteous life is inspired not by a need to be right before God but by a gratefulness for what God has already done for you.

There is therefore now no condemnation to
them which are in Christ Jesus, who walk
not after the flesh, but after the Spirit.

ROMANS 8:1

The end of Romans 8 is one of the most exquisitely victorious passages in the Bible. Bookmark it in your Bible so that anytime you feel as though you are caught in a losing battle you can be

reminded that in Christ you are more than a conqueror. Absolutely nothing has the power to separate you from the love of Christ. God alone is powerful enough to separate you from His love by deciding to take it away. But He has shown you through the sacrifice of His own Son that He will stop at nothing to be able to keep loving you. You are secure in His love and will be for eternity.

Nay, in all these things we are more than conquerors through him that loved us.
Romans 8:37

Day 224

NEHEMIAH 1:1–3:16
ROMANS 9:1–18
PSALM 119:65–72

Nehemiah is standing in the courts of the king, and the king asks him what he requests. What would be your knee-jerk reaction in this intimidating situation? Nehemiah's reaction was to pray. Even in the middle of the king's court, his dialogue with God continued. Nehemiah was constantly in the court of his heavenly King. Prayer is too often a second or third resort for us. Strive to be more like Nehemiah where the natural thing to do is to pray.

Then the king said unto me, For what dost thou make request? So I prayed to the God of heaven.

NEHEMIAH 2:4

℞omans 9:20 gives us an apt answer to a plethora of our doubting questions—who are we to reply to God? God's ways, thoughts, wisdom, and knowledge are so far above ours as to be incomprehensible to us. A dose of humility and trust in the love of God would do us good when facing life's hard questions.

Nehemiah 3:17–5:13
Romans 9:19–33
Psalm 119:73–80

Nay but, O man, who art thou that repliest against God? Shall the thing formed say to him that formed it, Why hast thou made me thus?

Romans 9:20

Day 226

NEHEMIAH 5:14–7:73
ROMANS 10:1–13
PSALM 119:81–88

*N*ehemiah 6:9 records a quick prayer that Nehemiah spoke to God in the face of fearful circumstances—"O God, strengthen my hands." We can probably assume that his life was punctuated perpetually with this type of prayer. He was in constant conversation with the One who was so much greater and more able than himself. May your thoughts be similarly inseparable from an inner conversation with your Father.

For they all made us afraid, saying, Their
hands shall be weakened from the work,
that it be not done. Now therefore,
O God, strengthen my hands.

NEHEMIAH 6:9

David had learned to delight in the Word of God. It had become his sustenance. In today's reading, he cited his knowledge of and delight in God's law as the reason he didn't perish in his

affliction. Knowing God's Word will keep you from falling, sustain your soul during grief, and bolster you with courage when you are afraid. It's through His Word that you can get to know God. Don't miss out on such a glorious opportunity.

Unless thy law had been my delights,
I should then have perished in mine affliction.
PSALM 119:92

Day 228

NEHEMIAH 9:6–10:27
ROMANS 11:25–12:8
PSALM 119:105–120

David asserted that God's Word was a lamp to his feet and a light to his path. If you are lacking direction in your life, go to God's Word. He has already provided you with the very light that you so crave to illuminate your future. Delve into this life-giving Word and seek to know all that you can from it. God will in turn use His Word to light your way. Use the lamp that He has provided.

Thy word is a lamp unto my feet,
and a light unto my path.

PSALM 119:105

Why is it that knowledge of spiritual matters often makes us feel arrogant? This is unacceptable. We are not to be wise in our own eyes. If we feel arrogant that we know God better

than someone else, then it's probably safe to say that we don't actually know Him at all. The God who humbled Himself to dwell and die on earth is not a God who takes delight in any form of arrogance or prejudice.

Be of the same mind one toward
another. Mind not high things,
but condescend to men of low estate.
Be not wise in your own conceits.
ROMANS 12:16

Day 230

Neh. 12:27–13:31
Romans 13:8–14:12
Psalm 119:129–136

It is astounding and convicting to read through Psalm 119 and see the immense love that David had for God's Word. As someone who was so intimately acquainted with God's laws and promises, it is no wonder that David was a man after God's own heart. His heart is displayed to us in His Word. We come to know and love Him more fully the more time we spend in it.

Thy testimonies are wonderful:
therefore doth my soul keep them.

Psalm 119:129

*B*iblical hope is not a vain wish for something that might happen but rather a steadfast faith in something that is sure to happen. God is the God of hope because He is the very author of our hope.

Without His work and His promises, there would be nothing sure in which to have faith. Along with Paul in Romans 15:13, ask that God would fill you with joy and peace so that you would overflow with hope through the Holy Spirit.

Now the God of hope fill you with all joy
and peace in believing, that ye may abound
in hope, through the power of the Holy Ghost.

ROMANS 15:13

Day 232

ESTHER 2:19–5:14
ROMANS 15:14–21
PSALM 119:153–168

God is not directly referenced in the book of Esther. Still, the evidence of His work is woven throughout the entire narrative. Even if you don't acknowledge or notice God's work directly, be confident that He is constantly working out His will for you. Just like Esther, He may place you in a situation that does not seem to have any correlation with His will. And yet, you'll find that He has put you there for a very specific reason. . . "for such a time as this."

For if thou altogether holdest thy peace at this time, then shall there enlargement and deliverance arise to the Jews from another place; but thou and thy father's house shall be destroyed: and who knoweth whether thou art come to the kingdom for such a time as this?

ESTHER 4:14

David professed that he had chosen God's precepts. Desiring to know and follow God's Word is a choice and a commitment. Sometimes we get so caught up in avoiding legalism that we allow a healthy diligence and obedience to slide. Make a commitment to read, memorize, and meditate on God's Word. You will only ever be blessed by this kind of commitment.

Let thine hand help me; for I have chosen thy precepts.

Psalm 119:173

Day 234

ESTHER 9–10
ROMANS 16
PSALM 120–122

*B*e wise in what is good and simple concerning evil. In today's culture, it often seems that we are more well versed in and familiar with what is evil than what is good. Yet Paul entreats the Romans to be simple concerning evil. Don't pursue knowledge of things that tear down, that promote violence or abuse, or that are simply worthless. Instead, do pursue knowledge of what is good and lovely and valuable. Be an expert in these things.

For your obedience is come abroad unto all men.
I am glad therefore on your behalf: but yet I
would have you wise unto that which is good,
and simple concerning evil.

ROMANS 16:19

J ob understood that God is wiser than he could ever be and that if God could give immense blessing, He also had every right to take it away. He understood that he came into the world with nothing and

that he could take nothing with him into the next life. He therefore had a loose hold on his earthly possessions and relationships. He chose to bless the name of the Lord even in the midst of unspeakable suffering.

And said, Naked came I out of my mother's womb, and naked shall I return thither: the LORD gave, and the LORD hath taken away; blessed be the name of the LORD.
JOB 1:21

Day 236

JOB 4–6
1 COR. 1:26–2:16
PSALM 124–125

God uses the weak, broken, and foolish things of the world for His purposes. We see this concept all throughout scripture. Just as a piece of pottery can only let light through if it has cracks, so too God's light shines more clearly through those who do not have it all together. When God chooses to use us for His kingdom, it is our brokenness and weakness that allow God's power to become all the more visible to those around us.

But God hath chosen the foolish things of the world to confound the wise; and God hath chosen the weak things of the world to confound the things which are mighty.

1 CORINTHIANS 1:27

$\mathcal{J}$ ob asked a very astute question in chapter 9: How can a man be just with God when he has nothing to bring to the table? The answer, of course, is Christ. Job obviously did not have the blessing of knowing

what Christ would do on the cross, and so his standing before God seemed rather hopeless based solely on his own merit. We have the immense privilege of living in the new covenant, having been justified by our faith in Christ based solely on God's grace. Christ answered for God's wrath so that we would never have to.

I know it is so of a truth: but how should man be just with God? If he will contend with him, he cannot answer him one of a thousand.

JOB 9:2–3

Day 238

Job 10–13
1 Cor. 4:1–13
Psalm 128–129

Paul knew of nothing against himself. Can you say the same of yourself? Do you strive to live a life where you can have a clear, guiltless conscience before God? You shouldn't strive for holiness as a way to be right before God, because you can never attain that on your own. Rather, your obedience should be a response to the grace that God has already shown you by making you clean before Him. You are already blameless in His eyes, so live that way.

For I know nothing by myself; yet am I not hereby justified: but he that judgeth me is the Lord.

1 Corinthians 4:4

$\int$ n today's passage, Paul explained to the Corinthians that he never intended for them not to associate with sinners. He asserts that as Christians we ought to be in the world, getting to know the sexually

immoral, greedy, and idolatrous. To not associate with these nonbelievers would be to miss the point of our pilgrimage here on earth. God's light shines the brightest when brought into the darker corners of the world.

I wrote unto you in an epistle not to company with fornicators: yet not altogether with the fornicators of this world, or with the covetous, or extortioners, or with idolaters; for then must ye needs go out of the world.

1 CORINTHIANS 5:9–10

Day 240

JOB 17–20
1 CORINTHIANS 6
PSALM 131

Job had a remarkably clear vision of God's coming to earth and the subsequent resurrection of his own body. How he knew that his Redeemer would one day stand on earth and that one day he would see God in his own body, we don't know. But God had provided him a priceless comfort in his suffering to know that this was not the end of his body and that his Redeemer would one day make all things right.

For I know that my redeemer liveth, and that
he shall stand at the latter day upon the earth:
and though after my skin worms destroy this
body, yet in my flesh I shall see God.

JOB 19:25–26

Job had a right understanding of suffering. He understood that through his trials God was polishing him as you would a dirty piece of priceless gold. Often it is the battering of trials that brings out the power of God that dwells in each of His children. We can all testify to knowing someone who has gone through immense trials but is all the stronger and more grounded in God because of them. The end result, a glittering piece of gold, is worth the process of polishing.

But he knoweth the way that I take: when he hath tried me, I shall come forth as gold.
JOB 23:10

Day 242

JOB 24–27
1 COR. 7:17–40
PSALM 133–134

*I*t is a good and pleasant thing for God's people to dwell together in unity. Relationships are hard. People will disagree and cause contentions. But the value of having fellowship with other believers is precious enough that we should be striving to live in peace and unity with our brothers and sisters as much as possible. God has given us one another to bolster, uphold, soothe, convict, and encourage. Don't miss out on the value of spending time with His people.

Behold, how good and how pleasant it is for brethren to dwell together in unity!

PSALM 133:1

In the whole scheme of things, we know so very little. It's true that the more we learn, the more we realize how little we know. So make it a priority to seek out the most valuable kind of knowledge.

Seek to know your God. Though our knowledge of God will always be limited in this life because of our finite minds, we are known perfectly by Him. He knows us better than we know ourselves.

And if any man think that he knoweth any thing,
he knoweth nothing yet as he ought to know.
But if any man love God, the same is known of him.

1 Corinthians 8:2–3

Day 244

Job 31–33
1 Cor. 9:1–18
Psalm 136:1–9

The refrain "for his mercy endureth for ever" occurs twenty-six times in Psalm 136. Each verse is punctuated by that phrase. Shouldn't our lives be punctuated by that refrain as well? After every chapter and verse of our lives, we can truthfully say, "His mercy endures forever." His mercy is woven all throughout the small, insignificant days as well as the life-changing events of our lives. It endures forever and will buoy us into the next life.

O give thanks unto the Lord; for he is good: for his mercy endureth for ever.

Psalm 136:1

Paul strove to reach as many people as he possibly could for the sake of the Gospel. His own sense of self or personal reputation was of no concern compared to the need he felt to tell people of Christ.

Day 245

Job 34–36
1 Cor. 9:19–10:13
Psalm 136:10–26

He became as a servant, as a Jew, as one under the Law, as one outside of the Law, and as weak in order to reach those in each category. The Gospel requires sacrifice and a giving up of oneself. But Paul would assert that this sacrifice was well worth it so that he could share in the riches of the Gospel with those he had reached.

To the weak became I as weak, that I might gain the weak: I am made all things to all men, that I might by all means save some. And this I do for the gospel's sake, that I might be partaker thereof with you.

1 Corinthians 9:22–23

Day 246

JOB 37–39
1 COR. 10:14–11:1
PSALM 137

When God speaks back to Job, it is an awe-inspiring, terrifying, and humbling thing to read. Imagine being there and seeing and hearing the power of God. How could we ever begin to think that we know better than God? Were we there when He created the earth? Do we hold the universe together from day to day? It has taken us millennia to even begin to discover the depths of the mysteries of this world that He created by simply speaking it into existence. And yet, we sometimes dare to assume that our will is better than His.

Where wast thou when I laid the foundations of the earth? declare, if thou hast understanding.

JOB 38:4

*J*ob's response to God is the only possible response to an encounter with God—complete and utter humility of oneself coupled with the utmost praise of God. Job's life would never have been the same

after this. Imagine how radically your life would change after having been directly spoken to by God. And yet, He has given us access to Himself every single day. Listen for His voice as you read His Word and pray. May it humble you and cause you to praise and magnify Him.

I know that thou canst do every thing,
and that no thought can be withholden
from thee. Who is he that hideth counsel
without knowledge? therefore have
I uttered that I understood not;
things too wonderful for me,
which I knew not.

JOB 42:2–3

Day 248

*E*cclesiastes is a remarkably apt description of life apart from God—life "under the sun." Apart from the purposes of God, all that we do on this earth is vanity and a passing shadow. God has put eternity in man's heart (Ecclesiastes 3:11) so that we inevitably realize that there has to be something more to life. Only a life that is lived with an "over the sun" perspective will provide true fulfillment and joy.

Vanity of vanities, saith the Preacher, vanity of vanities; all is vanity. What profit hath a man of all his labour which he taketh under the sun?

ECCLESIASTES 1:2–3

God formed you in the womb and knew you before anyone else was even aware of your existence. Before the first beat of your heart, He planned out a life for you in which you would have the unmatchable privilege of knowing Him. For Him to have spent this much thought on your life means that you are exceptionally valuable to Him. The opinions that people on earth may have of you are nothing compared to the opinion and love that God has for you.

Thine eyes did see my substance, yet being unperfect;
and in thy book all my members were written,
which in continuance were fashioned,
when as yet there was none of them.
Psalm 139:16

Day 250

Eccl. 7:1–9:12
1 Cor. 14:1–22
Psalm 139:19–24

*N*ow is the time to work hard, to invest in people's lives, and to seek after wisdom and knowledge. In heaven we won't have the opportunity to speak of God to the lost. In heaven we won't have the opportunity to bind up the broken and heal the sick. Obviously, the perfection of heaven is incomparably preferable to the fallen state of this world, but you should make the most of your time here. It will be all the chance you get to be a light for God in the darkness.

Whatsoever thy hand findeth to do, do it with thy might; for there is no work, nor device, nor knowledge, nor wisdom, in the grave, whither thou goest.

ECCLESIASTES 9:10

The conclusion of Solomon's study into life is this: "Fear God, and keep his commandments." God is the one who will ultimately bring judgment on all that you have done in life. His

Day 251

ECCL. 9:13–12:14
1 COR. 14:23–15:11
PSALM 140:1–8

opinion should be of the utmost concern to you. Your life should be lived to glorify and enjoy Him. Because in the end, the conclusion of your whole life will consist of what you have done for others and for the kingdom.

Let us hear the conclusion of the whole matter:
Fear God, and keep his commandments: for this
is the whole duty of man. For God shall bring
every work into judgment, with every secret thing,
whether it be good, or whether it be evil.

ECCLESIASTES 12:13–14

Day 252

Song of Sol. 1–4
1 Cor. 15:12–34
Psalm 140:9–13

*C*hristianity hinges on the reality of Christ's death and resurrection. Without the person of Jesus, your faith is worthless. It would be the easiest religion to disprove if only someone would have found the bones of Jesus. And yet, no one did because Christ rose from the dead, appeared to many people on earth, and currently sits on His throne in heaven. We have hope in Christ not only in this life but in the next as well. Instead of the most miserable of all people, we are the most blessed and should be the most grateful.

If in this life only we have hope in Christ,
we are of all men most miserable.

1 Corinthians 15:19

P salm 141:3 is a prayer that we should pray every day—*Lord, set a watch on my mouth and keep the door of my lips.* How much less trouble would we get into if our thoughts and words were always filtered through the grace of God? What if everything we said built others up and glorified Him? What if our thoughts were always pure and lovely? Ask God to protect your words and even your very thoughts.

Day 253

Song of Sol. 5–8
1 Cor.15:35–58
Psalm 141

Set a watch, O Lord, before my mouth;
keep the door of my lips.
Psalm 141:3

Day 254

ISAIAH 1–2
1 CORINTHIANS 16
PSALM 142

Verse 16 is a beautiful turning point in chapter 1 of Isaiah. The start of the chapter is desolate as God recounts all the evil that His people have done and how they have not served Him as they should. Verses 16 and 17 are a call to repentance—wash, put away evil, do well, relieve the oppressed. And then verse 18 is a refreshing picture of redemption—our scarlet sins will be washed as clean as snow. This is how the Lord deals with His people. He does not leave us in our sin.

Wash you, make you clean; put away the evil of your doings from before mine eyes; cease to do evil; learn to do well; seek judgment, relieve the oppressed, judge the fatherless, plead for the widow.

ISAIAH 1:16–17

God told a tale of a vineyard in Isaiah 5 as an analogy of His people. It is a heartbreaking look into God's relationship with a sinful and ungrateful nation. He lovingly planted and tended to the vineyard

Day 255

ISAIAH 3–5
2 COR.1:1–11
PSALM 143:1–6

only for it to rebel against Him. He then asked of the people, "What else could I have done for My vineyard?" God has poured out blessings on us, yet how often do we rebel against Him and bring forth the wild grapes of our rebellion instead of the fruit of our gratefulness?

And now, O inhabitants of Jerusalem, and men of Judah, judge, I pray you, betwixt me and my vineyard. What could have been done more to my vineyard, that I have not done in it? wherefore, when I looked that it should bring forth grapes, brought it forth wild grapes?

ISAIAH 5:3–4

Day 256

ISAIAH 6–8
2 COR. 1:12–2:4
PSALM 143:7–12

Isaiah saw God in all His terrifying and majestic glory. When God asked whom He should send, Isaiah immediately and emphatically replied, "Here am I; send me." This is the only possible reaction of someone who has seen God enthroned on high. To know that God sits on His throne in victory should inspire us to respond to His call to go and spread His Gospel as enthusiastically and unhesitatingly as Isaiah did.

Also I heard the voice of the Lord, saying,
Whom shall I send, and who will go for us?
Then said I, Here am I; send me.

ISAIAH 6:8

Who are you that God should take notice of you? How is it that a life that is a mere shadow in the scheme of history could be intimately cared for by God? But He does care for you more than  you even know. It is a remarkable and incomprehensible concept. If you could grasp how deeply God knows and loves you, would it change your life? We feel important if we know someone famous on earth whose life is of the same value as ours—how much more worthy should we feel that we know and are known by the almighty God? We should indeed be happy that God is our Lord.

Lord, what is man, that thou takest knowledge of him! or the son of man, that thou makest account of him! Man is like to vanity: his days are as a shadow that passeth away.
PSALM 144:3–4

Day 257

ISAIAH 9–10
2 COR. 2:5–17
PSALM 144

Day 258

Isaiah 11–13
2 Corinthians 3
Psalm 145

In Christ we have an unmatchable hope and a glorious assurance of eternal life. Because of this, we should be bold to speak of it. How can we keep such a gift to ourselves? Do you not feel sufficient enough to share the Gospel? The good news is that you aren't sufficient in yourself, which is why you must rely on the unsurpassable sufficiency of God (2 Corinthians 3:5). It's through His power that you can have the boldness to share His Word.

Seeing then that we have such hope,
we use great plainness of speech.

2 Corinthians 3:12

*G*od's power, as demonstrated in His ability to create and sustain the entire universe, is incomparable to anything we know. But unlike so many humans who use power for personal gain or superiority, God uses His power to help the oppressed, release the prisoner, feed the hungry, and care for the orphan and widow. His power and justice are never separated from His love, kindness, and mercy.

Which made heaven, and earth, the sea, and all that therein is: which keepeth truth for ever: which executeth judgment for the oppressed: which giveth food to the hungry. The LORD looseth the prisoners.

PSALM 146:6–7

Day 260

ISAIAH 17–19
2 CORINTHIANS 5
PSALM 147:1–11

Paul told the Corinthians that the love of Christ constrained (or compelled) him. What does it look like for Christ's love to compel you? Every action would be inspired by the love of Christ. Every word would seek to disperse His love to others. Every prayer would be said in the light of our standing before God, which was secured by His sacrificial love. You truly would no longer live for yourself but rather for Him who gave up His life so that you might live.

For the love of Christ constraineth us; because we thus judge, that if one died for all, then were all dead: and that he died for all, that they which live should not henceforth live unto themselves, but unto him which died for them, and rose again.

2 CORINTHIANS 5:14–15

The psalmist in today's reading praised God for having strengthened his gates. In order to allow them to open and close, the gates would inevitably be the weakest part of a fortified city.

Therefore, it was essential that the gates be strong. Have you identified what the weakest points are in your defense against the enemy? Where is it in your life that sin creeps in the easiest? Ask God to strengthen your gates and to help you be proactive in protecting those particular areas.

For he hath strengthened the bars of thy gates;
he hath blessed thy children within thee.

PSALM 147:13

Day 262

ISAIAH 24:1–26:19
2 CORINTHIANS 7
PSALM 148

Grief and sorrow over sin is good so far as it leads to repentance. Understanding the weightiness of sin and how abhorrent it is to God is essential as you strive to banish it from your life. But sorrow over sin that leads to undue guilt is not healthy. As a redeemed child of God, holding on to the guilt of sin is essentially not to accept Christ's work on the cross for you. When you sin, grieve over it, repent, and then accept God's grace and forgiveness.

For godly sorrow worketh repentance to salvation not to be repented of: but the sorrow of the world worketh death.

2 CORINTHIANS 7:10

Psalm 150 is a glorious picture of how all of God's creation should be and how it will be one day. One day everything that has breath will praise the Lord. In the meantime, our praise of Him should fill our lives and spill over into the lives of others. He is entirely worthy of all our praise. He is worthy simply because of who He is—the great God above all gods. But He is also worthy because of the wonderful things He has done for us. Praise Him now and continue to praise Him until all the earth and the entire universe joins in.

Let every thing that hath breath praise the LORD. Praise ye the LORD.
PSALM 150:6

Day 264

ISAIAH 29–30

2 CORINTHIANS 9

PROVERBS 1:1–9

Just as a loving parent will wait for a wayward child to behave, so too will God wait patiently to be gracious to you. He will not get fed up with you. You won't be able to try His patience beyond what He can handle. He desires that you walk with Him and keep His commandments. He will never give up on those who are His.

And therefore will the LORD wait, that he
may be gracious unto you, and therefore
will he be exalted, that he may have mercy
upon you: for the LORD is a God of judgment:
blessed are all they that wait for him.

ISAIAH 30:18

So often our greatest struggles are against intangible things like our thought life or wayward desires. Fortunately, God has provided us weapons with divine power, capable of fighting the most insidious of enemies. Ask that God might help you take every thought captive in obedience to Christ—imagine how different (and more productive) your thought life would be! God is powerful enough even to conquer your most private thoughts of insecurity, pride, lust, or fear.

(For the weapons of our warfare are not carnal, but mighty through God to the pulling down of strong holds;) casting down imaginations, and every high thing that exalteth itself against the knowledge of God, and bringing into captivity every thought to the obedience of Christ.

2 CORINTHIANS 10:4–5

Day 266

ISAIAH 34–36
2 CORINTHIANS 11
PROVERBS 1:23–26

Paul was not in the least concerned about keeping up personal appearances. In fact, if he were to boast, he would boast in the very things that most of us would desire to keep hidden. Embarrassing accounts of how he, the mighty apostle of God, had to be saved from situations in the most humble of ways were merely fodder for his message about God's power. Don't be afraid to tell the stories that make you "look bad" but showcase the goodness and power of God.

If I must needs glory, I will glory of the things which concern mine infirmities. . . . And through a window in a basket was I let down by the wall, and escaped his hands.

2 CORINTHIANS 11:30, 33

Those who reproach and revile God's people are really reproaching God Himself. Situations in which you are berated for being a Christian can make you feel very vulnerable and alone. But

remember in those circumstances that God is standing right there beside you, bearing the revilement with you. Though you may feel like the target, it is really the Holy One of Israel that those people are pitting themselves against. It may be easy to scorn another human, but taunting the Maker of heaven and earth is never a good idea.

Whom hast thou reproached and blasphemed? and against whom hast thou exalted thy voice, and lifted up thine eyes on high? even against the Holy One of Israel.

ISAIAH 37:23

Day 268

ISAIAH 39–40
2 COR. 12:11–13:14
PROVERBS 2:1–15

There is a beautiful juxtaposition in Isaiah 40:10–11 that speaks clearly of God's character. Verse 10 depicts a strong warrior king who comes to rule the earth with a strong arm. Verse 11 completely changes imagery and speaks of a caring shepherd who carries the lambs in His arms and gently leads His sheep. We serve a God who is so powerful that He conquered death and evil but so good and loving that He gently leads and cares for us. In His mighty arms can be found true protection and blissful rest.

Behold, the Lord GOD will come with strong hand, and his arm shall rule for him: behold, his reward is with him, and his work before him. He shall feed his flock like a shepherd: he shall gather the lambs with his arm, and carry them in his bosom, and shall gently lead those that are with young.

ISAIAH 40:10–11

God has chosen you. He set you aside as one of His children before the foundation of the world. There is nothing to fear when you grasp that your whole life was planned far in advance by a loving

Father. And in those times when fear is too strong to hold at bay, He holds you by the hand to reassure and strengthen you. Listen as He says to you, "Fear not; I will help you."

Thou whom I have taken from the ends of the earth, and called thee from the chief men thereof, and said unto thee, Thou art my servant; I have chosen thee, and not cast thee away. Fear thou not; for I am with thee: be not dismayed; for I am thy God: I will strengthen thee; yea, I will help thee; yea, I will uphold thee with the right hand of my righteousness. . . . For I the LORD thy God will hold thy right hand, saying unto thee, Fear not; I will help thee.

ISAIAH 41:9–10, 13

Day 270

Do you truly believe that you are precious in God's eyes? Do you believe that He loves you as fully as He says? Do you believe that He would go to the ends of the earth in order to bring you back? With the fallacy of love that we've all experienced in this world, it's sometimes easier not to believe that we can be perfectly and fully loved. And yet, your heavenly Father, who considers you precious, will prove His love for you as He ceaselessly seeks you to draw you to Himself.

Since thou wast precious in my sight, thou hast been honourable, and I have loved thee: therefore will I give men for thee, and people for thy life.

ISAIAH 43:4

The book of Proverbs has lots to say about wisdom—its value, how we should search for it, and how a wise person behaves. Why is wisdom so important? Because it is an attribute of God. In wisdom, God created the earth and established the universe. Attaining wisdom will make us more like God. To be more like God is truly of more value than any gold or jewels.

Day 271

ISAIAH 44:21–46:13
GALATIANS 3:1–18
PROVERBS 3:13–26

The LORD by wisdom hath founded the earth;
by understanding hath he established the heavens.
By his knowledge the depths are broken up,
and the clouds drop down the dew.

PROVERBS 3:19–20

Day 272

The idols that we so foolishly cling to are no match for God. We work so hard to develop and protect our idols. We hold on to them as something precious. But there is no chance that any of those things could prevail against God. All our idols and foolish sins will be cast down before the throne of Christ, and we will have no answer as to why we exchanged the unmatchable glory of God for a filthy and worthless idol.

Stand now with thine enchantments, and with the multitude of thy sorceries, wherein thou hast laboured from thy youth; if so be thou shalt be able to profit, if so be thou mayest prevail.

ISAIAH 47:12

Why do we fear the power and opinions of man? We get so caught up with people pleasing and appearances that we forget the One whom we should actually fear—the One who has the power to destroy or sustain, to curse or bless. Humans are inherently mortal. God is everlasting. Whose side would you rather be on?

Day 273

ISAIAH 49:14–51:23
GALATIANS 4:1–11
PROVERBS 4:1–19

I, even I, am he that comforteth you: who art thou, that thou shouldest be afraid of a man that shall die, and of the son of man which shall be made as grass; and forgettest the LORD thy maker, that hath stretched forth the heavens, and laid the foundations of the earth; and hast feared continually every day because of the fury of the oppressor, as if he were ready to destroy? and where is the fury of the oppressor?

ISAIAH 51:12–13

Day 274

ISAIAH 52–54
GALATIANS 4:12–31
PROVERBS 4:20–27

Be diligent to guard your heart. Don't fill it with worthless lusts and empty entertainment. Be more concerned about your own heart than anyone else's. Hate your sins more than the sins of your friends or family. How easily we fall into busying ourselves with accusing others while our own hearts are harboring sin. Be diligent over your own heart—the life that will overflow from a well-kept heart will in turn bring others to Christ.

Keep thy heart with all diligence;
for out of it are the issues of life.
PROVERBS 4:23

Stand firm in the freedom that you have in Christ. In what areas of your life do you tend to slip into legalism or moralism? You cannot possibly earn your salvation. Christ's work alone

Day 275

ISAIAH 55–57
GALATIANS 5
PROVERBS 5:1–14

is what grants you righteousness and salvation. If your equation for salvation is Christ plus anything else (good works, keeping the Ten Commandments, etc.), then you have lost your stand in Christ's freedom and have slipped into a false gospel. Our standing before God is based on a past action of Christ on the cross. Our obedience to God is an outworking of our gratefulness to Him for our salvation.

Stand fast therefore in the liberty wherewith Christ hath made us free, and be not entangled again with the yoke of bondage.

GALATIANS 5:1

Day 276

ISAIAH 58–59
GALATIANS 6
PROVERBS 5:15–23

God promises to bless, heal, and answer us and to grant us righteousness when we feed the hungry, bring the homeless into our homes, and clothe the naked. God's love and care for the needy is impossible to miss while reading through the Bible. His heart is fully turned toward those who have no voice of their own. If this is where His heart is, isn't it where your heart should be as well?

Is it not to deal thy bread to the hungry, and that thou bring the poor that are cast out to thy house? when thou seest the naked, that thou cover him; and that thou hide not thyself from thine own flesh? Then shall thy light break forth as the morning, and thine health shall spring forth speedily: and thy righteousness shall go before thee; the glory of the LORD shall be thy reward. Then shalt thou call, and the LORD shall answer; thou shalt cry, and he shall say, Here I am.

ISAIAH 58:7–9

*G*od chose you as His child before the foundations of the world were set. He has ordained that you be holy and without blame before Him. He planned far ahead of your physical birth that you would

be adopted as one of His children and fully invited into His family. He did all this simply because it pleased Him to do so. There is no ulterior motive or manipulation. A love this full and this pure is virtually impossible for us to comprehend but something for us to be grateful for every single day.

According as he hath chosen us in him before the foundation of the world, that we should be holy and without blame before him in love: having predestinated us unto the adoption of children by Jesus Christ to himself, according to the good pleasure of his will.

EPHESIANS 1:4–5

Day 278

Isaiah 63:1–65:16

Ephesians 2

Proverbs 6:6–19

*A*t the start of Ephesians 2 is a list of the things that God has done for you—loved you, made you alive, saved you, raised you up, and seated you with Christ. Why would He do all these things for you? Does He want something in return? The astounding and humbling answer comes in verse 7—He did all these things so that He might show you His grace and His kindness toward you. His desire is to shower you with love and grace. How undeserving we are to belong to a God who is so selflessly gracious to us.

That in the ages to come he might shew the exceeding riches of his grace in his kindness toward us through Christ Jesus.

EPHESIANS 2:7

Paul prayed that the Ephesians would know the love of Christ that surpasses knowledge. He wanted them to know the unknowable. Christ's love for us is so vast that our finite minds cannot grasp it. But to know even the smallest drop of this unknowable love would be life changing. Ask God to begin to help you comprehend His incomprehensible love.

And to know the love of Christ, which passeth knowledge, that ye might be filled with all the fulness of God.
EPHESIANS 3:19

Day 280

JEREMIAH 1—2
EPHESIANS 4:17—32
PROVERBS 6:27—35

God knew the entire plan He had for Jeremiah's life before he was even born. He knew him better than anyone would know him before he was even conceived. He was completely sovereign over his life. He is completely sovereign over yours as well. The same care with which He formed Jeremiah in the womb He used to form you. Take courage. God is fully aware of the circumstances in your life—He knew about them before they had even happened. You don't have to fill Him in or catch Him up—He is the perfect one to go to with your fears and petitions.

Before I formed thee in the belly I knew thee;
and before thou camest forth out of the womb
I sanctified thee, and I ordained thee
a prophet unto the nations.

JEREMIAH 1:5

$\mathcal{D}$on't even let yourself toy with the works of darkness. They are entirely unfruitful, worthless, and destructive. Instead of ignoring or trying to hide the sin in your life, expose it. Sin is strongest in the darkness; being exposed to the light will cause it to shrivel and weaken. Talk to other trustworthy Christians who can help you throw off the load of sin so that you can spend your time and effort pursuing works of righteousness.

*And have no fellowship with the unfruitful
works of darkness, but rather reprove them.*
EPHESIANS 5:11

Day 282

JEREMIAH 4:23–5:31
EPHESIANS 6
PROVERBS 7:6–27

How often do you consider the spiritual warfare that is raging at this very moment in the world? While it would be unfruitful to fixate on these thoughts, it is important to keep in mind the gravity of the battle at hand. Use prayer as a weapon against the powers and rulers of the darkness in this world. Work to spread God's light to conquer the darkness.

For we wrestle not against flesh and blood, but against principalities, against powers, against the rulers of the darkness of this world, against spiritual wickedness in high places.

EPHESIANS 6:12

God is a promise keeper. He has proven Himself as such throughout history. Because of this, you can trust Him fully to fulfill His promise that He will perfect the good work He has started in you. This means that no sin, guilt, or apathy can keep Him from working in your life. Thoughts of your own worthlessness have no room or authority in your heart and mind. God will make perfect His work that He started in you—you can count on it.

Being confident of this very thing, that he which hath begun a good work in you will perform it until the day of Jesus Christ.

PHILIPPIANS 1:6

Day 284

JEREMIAH 7:27–9:16

PHIL. 1:27–2:18

PROVERBS 8:12–21

You have daily opportunities to shine God's light into this crooked and perverse world. Something as simple as doing everything without grumbling or complaining makes it apparent to the watching world that there is something different about you. Conversely, to fit right into the world with its grumblings and disputes does absolutely nothing for the cause of Christ. Seek ways to be a light. Let the world know through the way you live that you are a child of God.

Do all things without murmurings and disputings: that ye may be blameless and harmless, the sons of God, without rebuke, in the midst of a crooked and perverse nation, among whom ye shine as lights in the world.

PHILIPPIANS 2:14–15

In what do you find your worth? In your strength? Athletic ability? Looks? Social status? Good works? Knowledge? Though all these things can be gifts from God, the only thing in which you should truly glory is knowing the Lord. When thinking about the blessings in your life, does knowing God typically make it on the list? It is a privilege beyond anything else we can experience on this earth. Work to be defined more by how well you know your Savior than by anything else.

Thus saith the Lord, Let not the wise man glory in his wisdom, neither let the mighty man glory in his might, let not the rich man glory in his riches: but let him that glorieth glory in this, that he understandeth and knoweth me, that I am the Lord which exercise lovingkindness, judgment, and righteousness, in the earth: for in these things I delight, saith the Lord.
JEREMIAH 9:23–24

Day 286

JER. 11:18–13:27
PHILIPPIANS 3
PROVERBS 9:1–6

The "famous" followers of Christ are not perfect people. Rather, they are people who are especially aware of their imperfections and who, because of their flaws, learn to rely more on Christ. They know that even when they stumble, they are covered by Christ's righteousness.

And be found in him, not having mine own righteousness, which is of the law, but that which is through the faith of Christ, the righteousness which is of God by faith.

PHILIPPIANS 3:9

Philippians 4:6 is not just a pleasant suggestion or a quaint platitude. It is a command—do not be anxious. Bring your prayers and supplications to God. Paul could give this command

because he was absolutely certain that worrying was of no benefit. He was also absolutely sure that no anxiety-producing situation was too big or difficult for God to handle. To be anxious is to question that God is doing the right thing in your life. There is, therefore, zero reason to be anxious because He is undoubtedly in control and doing the right thing. So, instead of worrying, carry your burdens to Him and drop them at His feet.

Be careful for nothing; but in every thing by prayer and supplication with thanksgiving let your requests be made known unto God.
PHILIPPIANS 4:6

Day 288

JEREMIAH 16–17
COLOSSIANS 1:1–23
PROVERBS 10:1–5

Paul did not cease to pray for the Colossians that they would be filled with knowledge and wisdom and that they would "walk worthy of the Lord" in good works. Is there anything that you care about enough to never cease to pray for it? Maybe start with this prayer in Colossians 1.

For this cause we also, since the day we heard it, do not cease to pray for you, and to desire that ye might be filled with the knowledge of his will in all wisdom and spiritual understanding; that ye might walk worthy of the Lord unto all pleasing, being fruitful in every good work, and increasing in the knowledge of God.

COLOSSIANS 1:9–10

Christ made a public spectacle of the devil on the cross. The devil must have thought that he had finally triumphed over God as he saw Christ hanging on the cross. Little did he know that

in that moment was his greatest loss. The curtain that had separated God from His people was torn in two, the dead were raised, and the very earth quaked under the weight of the victory of Christ. On that cross, any hold that the devil had over us was destroyed as the decree that documented our debt was nailed to the cross and erased by Christ's blood. In Christ's death and resurrection was His and our victory.

Blotting out the handwriting of ordinances that was against us, which was contrary to us, and took it out of the way, nailing it to his cross; and having spoiled principalities and powers, he made a shew of them openly, triumphing over them in it.

COLOSSIANS 2:14—15

Day 290

JEREMIAH 20:7–22:19
COLOSSIANS 2:16–3:4
PROVERBS 10:15–26

What is it to know God? God said that King Josiah knew Him because he pled the cause of the poor and needy. We could probably think of far more glamorous ways to know God. And yet, this is what God Himself says it means to know Him. Could His heart for those in need be any more clear? And could His call for you to minister to the poor and needy be any more obvious?

He judged the cause of the poor and needy;
then it was well with him: was not
this to know me? saith the LORD.

JEREMIAH 22:16

$\mathcal{L}$ et the peace of God rule in your hearts." You are not called to "make" the peace of God rule in your heart or even to "ask for" it. Rather, you only need to let it rule. God's peace already dwells in your heart. Stop trying to anxiously figure out your life, and instead, let His peace rule your every thought and action. Don't allow any room for doubt or fear to usurp the throne in your heart.

And let the peace of God rule in your hearts,
to the which also ye are called in one body;
and be ye thankful.
COLOSSIANS 3:15

Day 292

JEREMIAH 24–25
COLOSSIANS 4:2–18
PROVERBS 11:1–11

God gives you a heart to know Him. On your own you would be helpless in seeking out God. But He desires that you know Him, and He does not hide from you. He has given you all that you need to know Him. The Lord controls the hearts of everyone on this earth and can turn them wherever He chooses. If your heart is His, it always will be.

And I will give them an heart to know me,
that I am the Lord: and they shall be my
people, and I will be their God: for they shall
return unto me with their whole heart.

JEREMIAH 24:7

*H*ow many grudges, arguments, and lost relationships could have been avoided by concealing a matter? Gossip is often used to allay our own insecurities. If we can just get someone else to look bad, we assume that we'll look so much better. There are much more productive ways of dealing with insecurities. Dwell on how much you, as an image bearer, are loved by your Creator. And dwell even more on how much everyone around you is also highly valuable simply for bearing the image of their Father. Be a secret keeper and not a talebearer.

Jeremiah 26–27
1 Thess. 1:1–2:8
Proverbs 11:12–21

A talebearer revealeth secrets: but he that is
of a faithful spirit concealeth the matter.
Proverbs 11:13

Day 294

JEREMIAH 28–29
1 THESS. 2:9–3:13
PROVERBS 11:22–26

Paul prayed that the Thessalonians' love would increase for each other and for all people. Why? So that God would establish their hearts as blameless and holy at the coming of Christ. Love for one another is so central to the message of the Gospel. This is not a surface love that allows others to do whatever they want as long as it makes them happy, even if it's ultimately detrimental. Rather, it's a love that encourages and spurs each other on to live a blameless and holy life. How often do you think about the people you love standing in judgment before a holy God? Would that perspective change the way you love them here on earth?

And the Lord make you to increase and abound in love one toward another, and toward all men, even as we do toward you: to the end he may stablish your hearts unblameable in holiness before God, even our Father, at the coming of our Lord Jesus Christ with all his saints.

1 THESSALONIANS 3:12–13

$\mathcal{E}$ ven when God reprimands and punishes His children, He still loves them. In fact, it's because He loves His children that He rebukes them. But no matter what trials He may bring you through, His love is everlasting and therefore will not cease or fail you. With loving-kindness He will draw you in, and one day you will see the clearest evidence of His love threading all the way through your life, both in the trials and in the joys.

The LORD hath appeared of old unto me, saying,
Yea, I have loved thee with an everlasting love:
therefore with lovingkindness have I drawn thee.
JEREMIAH 31:3

Day 296

Jer. 31:23–32:35
1 Thess. 5:12–28
Proverbs 12:1–14

We all know the feeling of being let down, of watching promises be broken, of seeing expectations shattered. In this life we can expect to be disappointed and hurt. This is why it is so important that we have a God who will never fail us. He is perfectly and unwaveringly faithful. What He has promised to do He will do. No exceptions. It's in the chaos and uncertainty of this world that we begin to more fully appreciate the steadfastness of God.

Faithful is he that calleth you,
who also will do it.
1 Thessalonians 5:24

G od promises that if you call on Him, He will answer you. This in itself is a remarkable promise that the God of the universe will always answer you when you call on Him. But He doesn't just promise

to give a quick answer and then move on before you take up too much of His time. On the contrary, He will invest in you, guide and teach you, and show you great and mighty things. The amount of time and energy that God chooses to put into such insignificant creatures as ourselves is truly breathtaking.

Call unto me, and I will answer thee,
and show thee great and mighty
things, which thou knowest not.
JEREMIAH 33:3

Day 298

Do not grow weary in doing good. Doing good should not just be something on the side. It should be a lifestyle, something that defines who you are. The power of a kind word, a listening ear, or time taken out of your day for someone else should not be underestimated. Be hospitable. Reach out to the lonely and needy. Listen to the grieving. Serve as Christ served while He walked among us.

But ye, brethren, be not weary in well doing.

2 THESSALONIANS 3:13

*I*t's no mistake that in several places in the Bible emphasis is put on the dangers of what you say. Would you have fewer regrets in life had you faithfully kept your mouth as Solomon advises in Proverbs?

Life is the outcome for those who are wise and uplifting with their words. But destruction waits for those who use their words carelessly.

He that keepeth his mouth keepeth his life:
but he that openeth wide his lips
shall have destruction.
PROVERBS 13:3

Day 300

JEREMIAH 38:14–40:6
1 TIMOTHY 1:18–3:13
PROVERBS 13:5–13

Where does your wealth lie? Are you making yourself rich on things that amount to nothing? Or are you in possession of greater riches than this world could ever offer? The treasure that will last is your relationship with God and your investment in other people for the kingdom. These riches are those that are stored up in heaven. Everything else cannot come with you. Invest in the riches that will last into eternity.

There is that maketh himself rich, yet hath nothing: there is that maketh himself poor, yet hath great riches.

PROVERBS 13:7

P hysical exercise is healthy and good but is only profitable in this lifetime. Spiritual exercise is profitable not only in this lifetime but in the one to come. Put the same effort into spiritual

fitness as an Olympian would into physical fitness. Set aside time each morning for "training." Meditate on God's Word throughout the day. Recite God's Word to yourself as you fall asleep.

For bodily exercise profiteth little: but godliness is profitable unto all things, having promise of the life that now is, and of that which is to come.
1 TIMOTHY 4:8

Day 302

JEREMIAH 43–44
1 TIMOTHY 4:11–5:16
PROVERBS 13:22–25

Are you giving in to a sin that is killing you even while you live? God has promised you abundant life; don't throw that away for something that will only deaden your soul. Though we like to think that sin is a private matter, it almost inevitably affects more than just ourselves. Don't poison yourself and slowly suffocate the spirits of those around you for something worthless. Ask the giver of life to take away your desire for sin and in its place give you an all-consuming desire for Him.

But she that liveth in pleasure is dead while she liveth.

1 TIMOTHY 5:6

Paul's perspective on contentment is an excellent one. Why would we desire for more than we have when we are fully aware that just as we brought nothing into this world, we can

certainly take nothing out of it? Our simple sustenance and clothing is all that we really need. The rest of what we have is a blessing and a gift from God. Be grateful for what God has given you, but hold on to your worldly possessions with a loose hand, for the seed of discontent quickly grows into bitterness.

But godliness with contentment is great gain.
For we brought nothing into this world,
and it is certain we can carry nothing out.
And having food and raiment let
us be therewith content.
1 TIMOTHY 6:6–8

Day 304

JEREMIAH 48:1–49:6
2 TIMOTHY 1
PROVERBS 14:7–22

*C*hrist abolished death, having completely decimated it when He rose from the dead. Covered in His blood shed for you, death cannot touch you either. This means that you are immortal until the day that God has long ago appointed for you to go home to Him. And even then, death is nothing to fear, merely a necessary doorway into life everlasting—a passage through which Christ will walk with you as He has already walked before.

But is now made manifest by the appearing of our Saviour Jesus Christ, who hath abolished death, and hath brought life and immortality to light through the gospel.

2 TIMOTHY 1:10

Thank God that our lack of faith and obedience doesn't affect Him. Even when we are unfaithful and stumble badly, God remains entirely faithful and secure. Our sins do not mar Him since they are now and evermore carried in the scars of Jesus. For our sins Christ was sacrificed. By His wounds we are forgiven. Because God cannot deny Himself, this sacrifice was necessary. But because God is merciful beyond anything we deserve, He gave His Son in our place.

JEREMIAH 49:7–50:16
2 TIMOTHY 2
PROVERBS 14:23–27

If we believe not, yet he abideth faithful:
he cannot deny himself.

2 TIMOTHY 2:13

Day 306

Jer. 50:17–51:14
2 Timothy 3
Proverbs 14:28–35

*Y*our Redeemer is strong; the Lord of hosts is his name. There is no shortcoming on your part that He can't fill. There is no fear that He can't conquer. There is no wound that He can't heal. There is no grief that He can't assuage. There is no mourning that He can't turn into dancing. This is your God. He pleads your cause. Rest in Him.

Their Redeemer is strong; the Lord of hosts is his name: he shall throughly plead their cause, that he may give rest to the land, and disquiet the inhabitants of Babylon.

JEREMIAH 50:34

Paul recounted one of many times that the Lord stood by him. Christ stands by His people even though no one stood by Him in His hour of need. The abandonment and loneliness He felt on the cross is a grief and a pain that we can never imagine—nor will we ever have to since He bore it for us. We will never be forsaken, because He was. We will never be alone, because He was. We will never bear the just wrath of God, because He did. You can be confident that Christ will always stand by you because He does so based on no merit of your own.

Notwithstanding the Lord stood with me,
and strengthened me; that by me the
preaching might be fully known,
and that all the Gentiles might hear:
and I was delivered out of the
mouth of the lion.

2 TIMOTHY 4:17

Day 308

God cannot lie. This means that the promises and truths He speaks in His Word are fully reliable and trustworthy. He has promised eternal life to those who are His children. Therefore, as a child of God, you have a true and sure hope in eternal life with Him. This life and all its grief and sorrow is not even a drop in the ocean compared to the life of perfect joy and blessing that you have waiting for you.

In hope of eternal life, which God, that cannot lie,
promised before the world began.

Titus 1:2

This beautifully uplifting passage in Lamentations 3 is often taken out of context. It's easy to think that this sentiment was spoken by someone whose life was going well, who woke up every morning excited for a new day. But these precious verses are all the more beautiful because they were written from the pit of despair. This faith in God's daily compassion was held to in a dark place. These words were spoken by someone who clung to God's mercies as the only hope of life. No matter the darkness, God's light will find its way to you.

It is of the LORD's mercies that we are not consumed, because his compassions fail not. They are new every morning: great is thy faithfulness. The LORD is my portion, saith my soul; therefore will I hope in him.

LAMENTATIONS 3:22–24

Day 310

Lam. 3:39–5:22
Titus 3
Proverbs 15:27–33

"Think before you speak" may seem like a tired adage, but it's a valuable one nonetheless. A righteous person studies his answer before making a reply. A wicked person pours forth evil and worthless things with no thought or care. Whose speech do your words resemble more—the wicked, careless person or the righteous, mindful person?

The heart of the righteous studieth to answer: but the mouth of the wicked poureth out evil things.

Proverbs 15:28

$\mathcal{N}$o matter what plans you devise in your own heart regarding how your life should go, God is the One who ultimately guides your steps. He may (and often does) take you down a totally different

path than you had planned. The story of Onesimus in the book of Philemon is just one example of this. Onesimus left Philemon as a runaway slave and was commanded by Paul to return to Philemon as a fellow brother in Christ. It is doubtful that this was at all the plan that Onesimus had for his life when he ran away. But the story God crafted for him was more glorious than anything he could have devised.

A man's heart deviseth his way:
but the LORD directeth his steps.
PROVERBS 16:9

Day 312

Ezekiel 3:22–5:17
Hebrews 1:1–2:4
Proverbs 16:10–21

We cannot deny the Gospel. We cannot overlook the work of God that is so evident in the lives of the people whom He touches. We cannot reject the work of the Holy Spirit as He turns hearts of stone into hearts that fervently seek the Lord. We cannot escape the condemnation that comes to those who disavow their Creator who put His fingerprints so clearly over all creation. Only through accepting and embracing the work of Christ can you be truly free. Spread this essential news to all around you.

How shall we escape, if we neglect so great salvation; which at the first began to be spoken by the Lord, and was confirmed unto us by them that heard him; God also bearing them witness, both with signs and wonders, and with divers miracles, and gifts of the Holy Ghost, according to his own will?

HEBREWS 2:3–4

Death has no power in your life. The conqueror of death now rules in your heart, leaving no room for fear. The effects of death are temporary and fleeting and quickly give way to a more glorious reality. Christ has turned the devil's greatest weapon into His most beautiful gift, for through death is the doorway to a much better life.

Forasmuch then as the children are partakers of flesh and blood, he also himself likewise took part of the same; that through death he might destroy him that had the power of death, that is, the devil; and deliver them who through fear of death were all their lifetime subject to bondage.

HEBREWS 2:14–15

Day 314

EZEKIEL 8–10
HEBREWS 3:1–4:3
PROVERBS 17:1–5

*I*t is undeniably evident all throughout scripture that God defends and loves the poor and needy. As a God who is defined by love and justice, it's no wonder that He pays special attention to those who through injustice receive little love. Those who mistreat or mock the poor are really just mocking their Maker, which is an enormously bad idea. Those who speak up for and defend the poor become more like their Maker in that very act.

Whoso mocketh the poor reproacheth his Maker: and he that is glad at calamities shall not be unpunished.

PROVERBS 17:5

We are to come boldly to the throne of grace. Why? So that we might receive grace and mercy. If we need grace and mercy, then it means we are far from perfect. In our imperfection, what right do we

have to enter into the throne room of a holy God? And yet, God calls us to come—and to come boldly no less. Clearly, this is not an us-centered boldness based on what we have done and how clean our man-made robes are. Rather, it is a God-centered boldness based on what He has done and how clean the blood-washed, heavenly robes are that we have been given.

Let us therefore come boldly unto the throne of grace, that we may obtain mercy, and find grace to help in time of need.
Hebrews 4:16

Day 316

EZEKIEL 13–14
HEBREWS 5:11–6:20
PROVERBS 17:13–22

If a ship is moored by a trust-worthy anchor, it can only go a certain distance from that anchor. It may be tossed around by the wind and pummeled with waves, but the anchor will not let it break free and get pushed out into the ocean. So too the hope that we have in God will never allow us to drift out to sea. We may be tossed and battered by life's waves, but only within the confines of the anchor's reach. God has anchored our soul to Himself through Christ's work on the cross. No matter how big the waves get, we have a hope in something sure.

Which hope we have as an anchor of the soul, both sure and stedfast, and which entereth into that within the veil.

HEBREWS 6:19

*C*hrist intercedes for you. Have you ever really pondered that? As you would lift up in prayer a family member or friend that you care deeply about, so too Christ, your truest friend, intercedes for

you to the Father. You could not ask for a better advocate. He has been where you have been and has seen and felt the weight of this world. That the Son of God would know how your suffering feels is astonishing. He is deeply connected to your human needs and desires. Having been your sacrificial Lamb, He is now and forever will be your High Priest.

But this man, because he continueth ever, hath an unchangeable priesthood. Wherefore he is able also to save them to the uttermost that come unto God by him, seeing he ever liveth to make intercession for them.

HEBREWS 7:24–25

Day 318

We often comfortably compare ourselves with Sodom, knowing that we are far more holy than the people living there who were truly evil and debased. And yet, what are the sins cited against Sodom? Pride, careless prosperity, idleness, and an inattention to the poor and needy. . . All of a sudden this seems a little uncomfortable. Is your life free of these sins? Just like the people of Sodom, we are wretched sinners whom God has every right to do away with. But He chose to redeem us and make us one of His family instead. Praise be to Him!

Behold, this was the iniquity of thy sister Sodom, pride, fulness of bread, and abundance of idleness was in her and in her daughters, neither did she strengthen the hand of the poor and needy. And they were haughty, and committed abomination before me: therefore I took them away as I saw good.

EZEKIEL 16:49–50

We have all heard the accusation that God is not fair. In fact, maybe you've thought that at times in your life. But how do we have any right to say that God's ways are not fair? To begin with, we can't even come close to comprehending the plans that God has for us. Also, we have done nothing for God compared to the matchless gifts and grace that He has given us. With all our fickleness, lack of gratefulness, and idolatry, we are the ones who are not fair.

Yet ye say, The way of the LORD is not equal. Hear now, O house of Israel; Is not my way equal? are not your ways unequal?
EZEKIEL 18:25

Day 320

Ezekiel 20
Hebrews 10:1–25
Proverbs 18:18–24

*C*hrist sat down at the right hand of God. The action of sitting down signified that His work was completed. It was finished. Unlike the other priests who would have to continually offer sacrifices, Christ's sacrifice was so powerful it put an end to the need for any further sacrifices. His work is finished, which means that your sins are already paid for. There is nothing that you have done that will fall outside the boundaries of His atoning sacrifice.

But this man, after he had offered one sacrifice for sins for ever, sat down on the right hand of God.

HEBREWS 10:12

God's love fully encompasses who He is. But to only consider that He is a loving God is to truncate your knowledge of Him, to diminish His glory, and ultimately to lack a full understanding of His love. God

is also a God who can be moved to wrath. He is a God to be feared in all His unattainable holiness. He can either create or destroy with a simple word. Knowing the power and fearfulness of God only makes the truth that He loves and cares for you more glorious.

It is a fearful thing to fall into the hands of the living God.
HEBREWS 10:31

Day 322

Ezekiel 23
Hebrews 11:1–31
Proverbs 19:9–14

Would those who interact with you on a daily basis recognize that you seek a homeland that is not of this world? Does your anticipation of your true home seep into your words and actions so much that it inspires others to seek this kingdom as well? What are you doing to seek out this heavenly land of which you are a citizen? Just as refugees on this earth often surround themselves with the comforts and reminders of their country of origin, so too remind yourself often of where you are going.

For they that say such things declare plainly that they seek a country. . . . But now they desire a better country, that is, an heavenly: wherefore God is not ashamed to be called their God: for he hath prepared for them a city.

HEBREWS 11:14, 16

In Hebrews 11 is a small parenthetical phrase that just may be the most powerful words ever put into parentheses—"Of whom the world was not worthy." This comfort-driven world is not worthy of people who will gladly be killed, beaten, and exiled so that they might follow their Savior. This selfish world is not worthy of people who value their lives so lightly that they would give them up for the sake of another. This compromising world is not worthy of people who refuse to budge an inch on the truth of the Gospel even when this steadfastness will cost them in this life. This world is not worthy of them. . .but they are worthy of their homes in heaven where every day they will dine with the Savior they so faithfully followed.

(Of whom the world was not worthy.)
Hebrews 11:38

Day 324

Ezekiel 27–28
Hebrews 12:1–13
Proverbs 19:22–29

*C*hastisement and discipline from God are not things that we generally look forward to. And yet, to not be disciplined is far worse. God will inevitably reprimand His children—it is how He lovingly makes us more like Himself. If you have not been corrected by Him, the sobering truth is that you may not truly be a child of His. Though it may seem a bit frightening, ask for God to make you more like Himself no matter what it takes—for it is far better to be one of His children than an outsider to His family.

But if ye be without chastisement, whereof all are partakers, then are ye bastards, and not sons.

Hebrews 12:8

Be careful to avoid being the kind of person who proclaims your own goodness but in whom none of this proclaimed goodness can be found. Rather, be the kind of person who doesn't speak much of yourself but, through your actions and character, proves yourself a faithful person. Be more concerned about building others up. Humbly let your praise come from God or others.

Most men will proclaim every one his own goodness: but a faithful man who can find?

PROVERBS 20:6

Day 326

EZEKIEL 31–32
HEBREWS 13
PROVERBS 20:19–24

*A*re you willing to bear the reproach of Jesus and go with Him outside the camp? Christians often find that they are not welcome in the upper reaches of society or the inner circles of secular culture. And yet, should we be surprised when we serve a Savior who suffered outside the gate? An outcast life with Him is far better than a thousand lives of earthly comfort without Him. No suffering can compare with the joy that He offers.

Wherefore Jesus also, that he might sanctify the people with his own blood, suffered without the gate. Let us go forth therefore unto him without the camp, bearing his reproach.

HEBREWS 13:12–13

W hat would you say is pure and undefiled religion? James says that pure religion is visiting the fatherless and widows in their distress and keeping yourself unstained from the world. This is likely not the first answer that we would come up with. And yet, it is what God calls us to. If you aren't caring for those in need, is your heart where it should be? Are you serving God as you ought to serve Him?

Pure religion and undefiled before God and the Father is this, To visit the fatherless and widows in their affliction, and to keep himself unspotted from the world.
JAMES 1:27

Day 328

Ezekiel 34:11–36:15
James 2
Proverbs 21:1–8

While good works by no means secure your salvation, they are an excellent barometer regarding your faith. A faith that is not played out in and invigorated by works is a faith that may not be genuine. The God in whom you have faith is a God who daily reaches out to and sustains His people, orchestrating every aspect of their lives. He is a God who is constantly working for our good. If your faith in this God is not similarly accented by working for others, then maybe you do not know your God as you should. Our good works are one of the most obvious ways that we can imitate Christ on this earth and reach others for Him. Let us not be people with a skeletal faith.

Even so faith, if it hath not works,
is dead, being alone.

James 2:17

*E*zekiel is mostly a very desolate book. God does not treat sin lightly—the punishment for ignoring the law of God is real. The intensity of the book makes the passages about God's redemption stand out all the more vividly. Even when your life feels desolate, God's Spirit remains alive and active within you. He does not abandon His people in the desert. He will bring you into a new and vibrant land. It's the experiences of being drawn out of the desert that cause us to look back and recognize that it is the Lord at work in us.

And shall put my spirit in you, and ye shall live, and I shall place you in your own land: then shall ye know that I the Lord *have spoken it, and performed it, saith the* Lord.

Ezekiel 37:14

Day 330

EZEKIEL 38–39
JAMES 4:1–5:6
PROVERBS 21:19–24

How often do we ask for something simply for our own comfort or pleasure without regard to how it will fit into God's kingdom plan or how it will affect others? We are masters at molding our idea of God's will to fit perfectly into our pre-constructed plan for our lives. Would your prayers sound different if your greatest desire was to be of use to God's kingdom? Would your prayers sound different if your first thought was toward others rather than yourself?

Ye ask, and receive not, because ye ask amiss,
that ye may consume it upon your lusts.

JAMES 4:3

*Y*ou are to establish your heart to prepare for the coming of Christ. Just as a tree needs water and nutrients for its roots to grow, so you also must feed your heart with the sustenance from God's

Word so that your spiritual roots will burrow down into a deeper relationship with Him. Bask in the light of His presence that you may be filled up with His joy.

Be ye also patient; stablish your hearts:
for the coming of the Lord draweth nigh.
JAMES 5:8

Day 332

Ezekiel 41:1–43:12
1 Peter 1:1–12
Proverbs 22:1–9

The kind of inheritance that we should be working for in this life is the one that is being stored up in heaven for us as an incorruptible, undefiled, and everlasting reward. This inheritance has nothing to do with money, ease of life, or status. Our heavenly inheritance is based on what our Father has already done for us and consists of riches beyond our imaginings. Our inheritance is sure because God Himself keeps us by His power and will grant us this inheritance based on no merit of our own.

To an inheritance incorruptible, and undefiled, and that fadeth not away, reserved in heaven for you, who are kept by the power of God through faith unto salvation ready to be revealed in the last time.

1 Peter 1:4–5

*Y*ou are called to be holy just as God is holy. This is a high and daunting calling. You will certainly fall short of it aside from the atoning work of Christ. But sometimes we use an avoidance of legalism as an excuse to not even try to be holy. While we certainly can't muster holiness on our own, this is no excuse not to strive for it in this life. The purity of our lives is one way that God shows Himself to those around us. The brokenness of our lives is how God reminds us of our need for Him. Both our striving for holiness and our admittance of our weakness are important factors in God's work in our lives.

But as he which hath called you is holy,
so be ye holy in all manner of conversation;
because it is written, Be ye holy; for I am holy.
1 Peter 1:15–16

Day 334

EZEKIEL 45–46
1 PETER 2:4–17
PROVERBS 22:24–29

First Peter 2:17 is a good and simple summation of how we ought to live our lives. Honor all people as image bearers of God, and in so doing, seek to serve them and bring them to Christ. Love your fellow Christians in a self-sacrificial way as Christ has taught us to do by His example. Fear God as the just and holy God who has every right to punish us for our sin but who has mercifully chosen to redeem us instead. Honor those placed in authority over you, and live as an upright and obedient citizen of this temporary home as much as you can while still obeying the law of God as your utmost authority.

Honour all men. Love the brotherhood.
Fear God. Honour the king.
1 PETER 2:17

The city spoken of in Ezekiel was named "The Lord is there." May our lives and homes be worthy of such a name as well. When others look in on your family or your personal life, will they recognize that God dwells with you? Does your life speak of the presence and redeeming work of God?

It was round about eighteen thousand measures: and the name of the city from that day shall be, The Lord is there.
EZEKIEL 48:35

Day 336

Daniel's first reaction to his answered prayer was to praise God. How often do you forget to praise God after He's answered a prayer? How often do you end up attributing the answer to your own intelligence or ability? We should live in an attitude of praise and gratefulness to God as He is constantly answering our prayers and granting us mercies that we didn't even think to pray for. He deserves the credit. Every good thing in our lives is ultimately a gift from Him.

Then was the secret revealed unto Daniel in a night vision. Then Daniel blessed the God of heaven.

DANIEL 2:19

The story of Shadrach, Meshach, and Abednego in the fiery furnace is a beautiful illustration of how Christ walks with us through trials. He does not abandon those who have been faithful to proclaim Him. Though we can't always see it, we are never alone. Oh, that God would open our eyes so that we could see that one "like the Son of God" walks by our side when we're in the midst of the fire.

He answered and said, Lo, I see four men loose, walking in the midst of the fire, and they have no hurt; and the form of the fourth is like the Son of God.
DANIEL 3:25

Day 338

DANIEL 4
2 PETER 1
PROVERBS 23:26–35

*A*s captives in Babylon, God's people must have felt that God had abandoned them or that He had somehow messed up His plan. They likely thought that maybe God wasn't sovereign after all. But they probably never would have imagined that God would use this very difficult circumstance to bring a pagan king into relationship with Himself. We can never possibly know what it is that God plans to do through the hard circumstances that He puts us in. We must tirelessly trust in His sovereignty and grace and believe that He does have a better plan than ours.

And at the end of the days I Nebuchadnezzar lifted up mine eyes unto heaven, and mine understanding returned unto me, and I blessed the most High, and I praised and honoured him that liveth for ever, whose dominion is an everlasting dominion, and his kingdom is from generation to generation.

DANIEL 4:34

*F*alse teaching and the warping of God's truth to fit our own lifestyles is a serious offense to God and something that He does not take lightly. He is gracious enough to hate and punish false teaching

because to let us adhere to lies would ultimately destroy us. Be careful to test the teaching that you receive against the perfect Word of God. If it doesn't match up, side every time with the Word of God.

These are wells without water, clouds that are carried with a tempest; to whom the mist of darkness is reserved for ever.

2 PETER 2:17

Day 340

Daniel's enemies were fully aware that they could bring no accusation against him unless they could somehow use his unwavering faithfulness to God against him. What a testimony that is! Daniel was upright and pure in all his morals and obedience to the good laws of the land. He had no secret sin that could be used against him. He had not slightly bent or ignored any laws that could be brought to light as a witness against him. Could you say the same about yourself? Perhaps even more poignantly, his relationship with God was so well known that his enemies knew that he would never bend in regard to his faithfulness to God. Could you say the same about yourself?

Then said these men, We shall not find any occasion against this Daniel, except we find it against him concerning the law of his God.

DANIEL 6:5

There is no reason not to confess your sins to God. If you don't confess your sins, and deny that they exist, then they become witnesses against you that God's truth does not dwell in you.

Day 341

DANIEL 7:15–8:27
1 JOHN 1:1–2:17
PROVERBS 24:28–34

For His truth will inevitably reveal to us how we fail to keep His law. But if you confess your sins, they are guaranteed to be forgiven so that you can live with a clear conscience before God. With this in mind, why would you not daily confess your sins to your faithful Father?

If we say that we have no sin, we deceive ourselves, and the truth is not in us. If we confess our sins, he is faithful and just to forgive us our sins, and to cleanse us from all unrighteousness.

1 JOHN 1:8–9

Day 342

DANIEL 9–10
1 JOHN 2:18–29
PROVERBS 25:1–12

*B*ecause God is righteous and faithful, He must punish sin. If He chose to let an indiscretion slide here or there or simply pretended that He didn't see a sin, He could not be trusted. An unfaithful or fickle god is not one that you would want to put your trust in. It's His very wrath and justice that make Him trustworthy. Because of God's holiness, sin needs to be punished—you ought to be eternally grateful that the punishment fell on Christ instead of you. It was inevitable that the blow would fall, but God is incomprehensibly gracious, having taken the blow onto Himself rather than put it on those who truly deserved it.

Therefore hath the LORD watched upon the evil, and brought it upon us: for the LORD our God is righteous in all his works which he doeth: for we obeyed not his voice.

DANIEL 9:14

*Y*ou can almost sense the wonder in John's words about the gift of being called a child of God. We should have the same wonder, as well, that the Creator of all things would bestow on us the honor and

Day 343
DANIEL 11–12
1 JOHN 3:1–12
PROVERBS 25:13–17

privilege of being one of His children. He redeemed and justified us so that we would be spared the punishment of sin. But the truly remarkable thing is that He didn't stop there. He went so far as to adopt us. In this adoption He identifies with us and puts the stamp on us that we belong forever to Him. This manner of love is one that is impossible to comprehend.

Behold, what manner of love the Father hath
bestowed upon us, that we should be called
the sons of God: therefore the world knoweth
us not, because it knew him not.
1 JOHN 3:1

Day 344

HOSEA 1–3
1 JOHN 3:13–4:16
PROVERBS 25:18–28

*I*n Hosea is depicted a painfully beautiful story that is analogous to God's relationship with us. God has betrothed Himself to us and will therefore continue to seek us out no matter how many times we spit in the face of His faithfulness. We may run from Him. We may muddy His reputation by the worthless and soul-destroying sins that we continue to pursue as though they are more precious to us than our relationship to Him. Even in the face of this heartbreaking betrayal, He lovingly draws us back to Himself. To say that we don't deserve this kind of love is a huge understatement.

And I will betroth thee unto me for ever; yea, I will betroth thee unto me in righteousness, and in judgment, and in lovingkindness, and in mercies. I will even betroth thee unto me in faithfulness: and thou shalt know the LORD.

HOSEA 2:19–20

Because of our faith in Christ, we have overcome the world. This means that, being hidden in His wings, nothing on this earth can touch us. There is no power or darkness that could come close to pulling us away from Christ or darkening the light of His presence in our hearts. Christ defeated the powers of this fallen world. Since He lives in us, we have become conquerors as well. Live in light of your victory over the sins and enticements of this world.

---

*For whatsoever is born of God overcometh the world:
and this is the victory that overcometh the world,
even our faith. Who is he that overcometh the world,
but he that believeth that Jesus is the Son of God?*

1 John 5:4–5

Day 346

Hosea 7–10
2 John
Proverbs 26:17–21

The book of Proverbs is fascinating in how accurately it identifies human character. Not much has changed in the way we behave in the centuries since it was written. Do you see yourself in any of the descriptions? For instance, one of Solomon's warnings is against people who are rude and hurtful to someone and then cover themselves by saying, "I was only joking." Solomon compared a person that does this to a madman who casts death. This kind of deception and carelessness is not something to be taken lightly.

As a mad man who casteth firebrands, arrows, and death, so is the man that deceiveth his neighbour, and saith, Am not I in sport?

Proverbs 26:18–19

*F*ollow and imitate what is good. When you do good, you are like God because God is good and only does what is good for His people. Surround yourself with people who are already doing good and working hard for God's kingdom and then imitate these people. By imitating others who are already walking in a way worthy of their God, you are really imitating Christ. The more Christlike you become, the more abhorrent evil will be, and the more wholeheartedly you will strive to do good.

Beloved, follow not that which is evil, but that which is good. He that doeth good is of God: but he that doeth evil hath not seen God.

3 JOHN 1:11

Day 348

JOEL 1:1–2:17
JUDE
PROVERBS 27:10–17

God is able to keep you from falling and to present you faultless before God in glory. This certainly sounds nice, but do you really believe it? Have you let this truth seep into your thoughts about yourself? Under God's care you will not fall. Nothing you can do will mar the perfection of Jesus' robes that you are covered in. Not only will you be blameless at the final judgment, but you will actually be able to stand before the most holy and just God with joy—that is how confident you will be in the work that Christ has accomplished for you. Live in that freedom and confidence here and now.

Now unto him that is able to keep you from falling, and to present you faultless before the presence of his glory with exceeding joy, to the only wise God our Saviour, be glory and majesty, dominion and power, both now and ever. Amen.

JUDE 1:24–25

*G*od is the Alpha and the Omega. He is the beginning and the ending of the entire stretch of history. He is the prologue and epilogue to all eternity. He has always and will always exist. Can you imagine anyone better in whom to put your trust? No matter who may disappoint or desert you in this life, your God is present beside you and will remain so throughout eternity. You will never know a day in which your heavenly Father is not caring for you.

I am Alpha and Omega, the beginning and the ending, saith the Lord, which is, and which was, and which is to come, the Almighty.
REVELATION 1:8

Day 350

Amos 1:1–4:5
Revelation 2:12–29
Proverbs 28:1–8

The Spirit commended the church of Pergamum for holding fast to God's name even though they dwelled where Satan's throne was. Though He goes on to point out some things that the church was not doing well, it remains a beautiful testimony that this faithful church was shining Christ's light into the darkest of places. They stood strong at the very gates of hell. They proclaimed Christ as victor over all the earth, even the parts where Satan's power seemed overwhelming.

I know thy works, and where thou dwellest, even where Satan's seat is: and thou holdest fast my name, and hast not denied my faith, even in those days wherein Antipas was my faithful martyr, who was slain among you, where Satan dwelleth.

REVELATION 2:13

Take an inventory of your true, everlasting riches versus your false, fleeting riches. Sometimes earthly wealth lulls us into thinking that we are safe and secure. But apart from the riches that only come through a personal relationship with Christ, we are wretched, miserable, poor, blind, and naked. Seek the true riches that Christ offers you.

Because thou sayest, I am rich, and increased with goods, and have need of nothing; and knowest not that thou art wretched, and miserable, and poor, and blind, and naked.

REVELATION 3:17

Day 352

Amos 7–9
Revelation 4:1–5:5
Proverbs 28:17–24

The four living creatures in heaven constantly proclaim, "Holy, holy, holy, Lord God Almighty, which was, and is, and is to come." They do not rest from their praise of their Maker. Though God has put us on this earth for a different purpose than to proclaim His holiness without ceasing, it is still of value to consider how often you praise God. Even if you aren't constantly speaking of His greatness, your life can still proclaim His perfect work in you. And one day we will join in this endless praise, because to encounter the Lord in all His holiness is to inevitably be inspired to praise Him.

And the four beasts had each of them six wings about him; and they were full of eyes within: and they rest not day and night, saying, Holy, holy, holy, Lord God Almighty, which was, and is, and is to come.

Revelation 4:8

*I*n his vision, John stood weeping because he saw no one who could open the scroll. But then one of the elders assured him that the Lion of Judah had the authority to open the scroll. We look with anticipation to

see this Lion, but what does John see by the throne? A slain Lamb. What beautiful imagery that this conquering Lion is displayed in all His power and glory as a sacrificed Lamb. In His completely counterintuitive and glorious plan, God sent His most powerful weapon, a humble sacrifice, to conquer the world, death, and all the powers of darkness.

And I beheld, and, lo, in the midst of the throne and of the four beasts, and in the midst of the elders, stood a Lamb as it had been slain, having seven horns and seven eyes, which are the seven Spirits of God sent forth into all the earth.

Revelation 5:6

Day 354

MICAH 1:1–4:5

REVELATION 6:1–7:8

PROVERBS 29:1–8

What a beautiful picture Micah prophesied, that every person will sit peacefully under their tree with absolutely nothing to make them afraid. Imagine a world in which nothing could make you afraid. This is the world that we get to look forward to in eternity. And even during this life, there is nothing that can make us afraid if we truly grasp the status that we have before God. The Lord of hosts has spoken that you are one of His forever-kept children. With this perspective, fear has no place in your heart or mind.

But they shall sit every man under his vine and under his fig tree; and none shall make them afraid: for the mouth of the LORD of hosts hath spoken it.

MICAH 4:4

Verses 6 and 7 of Micah 6 lay out increasingly costly scenarios of ways to pay for our sins. The last one Micah suggested almost incredulously, as it would be too much to bear—"shall I give my firstborn for my transgression?" And yet, this is exactly what the Lord has done for you. Since He did not desire to ask such a heart-wrenching sacrifice of you, He did it instead. Micah went on to lay out what God requires of us. We are simply to do justly, love mercy, and walk humbly with Him—He's done the rest for us.

Wherewith shall I come before the Lord, and bow myself before the high God? . . . Will the LORD be pleased with thousands of rams, or with ten thousands of rivers of oil? shall I give my firstborn for my transgression, the fruit of my body for the sin of my soul? He hath shewed thee, O man, what is good; and what doth the LORD require of thee, but to do justly, and to love mercy, and to walk humbly with thy God?

MICAH 6:6–8

Day 356

The book of Nahum starts out aggressively depicting God's power and wrath against offending nations. It gives us a good picture of why we ought to fear God. And then verse 6 abruptly switches gears to talk about the goodness of the Lord and how He is a stronghold in the day of trouble. How reassuring in the face of His wrath to be reminded that He knows and cares for those who trust in Him. In the midst of whirling chaos, He is ever your stronghold.

Who can stand before his indignation? and who can abide in the fierceness of his anger? his fury is poured out like fire, and the rocks are thrown down by him. The Lord is good, a strong hold in the day of trouble; and he knoweth them that trust in him.

NAHUM 1:6–7

Habakkuk was a man of true resilience. Was this because he was especially powerful or well-off or had a good network of support? No, it was because no matter what the circumstance, he had made the choice to rejoice in the Lord. His was a God-based prosperity, not a circumstance-based prosperity. For this reason, no negative earthly circumstance could touch him because no amount of failed crops or empty stalls would change his opinion of his God. His joy lay in his Savior, not his stuff.

Although the fig tree shall not blossom, neither shall fruit be in the vines; the labour of the olive shall fail, and the fields shall yield no meat; the flock shall be cut off from the fold, and there shall be no herd in the stalls: yet I will rejoice in the LORD, I will joy in the God of my salvation.

HABAKKUK 3:17–18

Day 358

ZEPHANIAH
REVELATION 12
PROVERBS 30:1–6

The Lord rejoices over you with singing. Can you believe that? Can you imagine that a God who created the universe, constantly sustains it, and listens to the prayers of billions of people every day rejoices over you? Insecurities, self-abasing self-talk, and low self-image have no place in the mind of someone who is rejoiced over by God. People will let you down and make you feel small and worthless, but when this happens, never forget that God continues to rejoice over you with joy and singing. Doesn't His opinion count for so much more than the opinion of anyone else?

The LORD thy God in the midst of thee is mighty;
he will save, he will rejoice over thee with joy; he will
rest in his love, he will joy over thee with singing.

ZEPHANIAH 3:17

ay God be so gracious that He gives us just the right amount of material wealth and comfort so that we continue to rely on and bless Him. May He be gracious enough to grant us contentment no matter what the circumstance. May our lives not be defined by vanity or treachery to get ahead in life, but rather, may they be lives of satisfaction in God alone without regard to material circumstances.

Day 359

HAGGAI
REV. 13:1–14:13
PROVERBS 30:7–16

Two things have I required of thee; deny me them not before I die: remove far from me vanity and lies: give me neither poverty nor riches; feed me with food convenient for me.

PROVERBS 30:7–8

Day 360

ZECHARIAH 1–4
REV. 14:14–16:3
PROVERBS 30:17–20

Do not despise small beginnings. Do you ever have visions of what you want to be or do for God's kingdom? Then when you take stock of your current life, what you're doing seems so insignificant it's almost worthless? God uses small beginnings to make big movements in His kingdom. Who knows how He will use your faithful steps today? Take courage that nothing is wasted in God's economy.

For who hath despised the day of small things?
for they shall rejoice, and shall see the plummet
in the hand of Zerubbabel with those seven;
they are the eyes of the LORD, which run to
and fro through the whole earth.

ZECHARIAH 4:10

God's fingerprints are all over His creation. His character can be found in His creativity. Since He is the author of all living things, it makes sense that even the smallest of creatures can speak of

His wisdom. Learn from the beautiful creation that He has given us to enjoy.

There be four things which are little upon the earth, but they are exceeding wise: the ants are a people not strong, yet they prepare their meat in the summer; the conies are but a feeble folk, yet make they their houses in the rocks; the locusts have no king, yet go they forth all of them by bands; the spider taketh hold with her hands, and is in kings' palaces.

Proverbs 30:24–28

Day 362

ZECHARIAH 9–11
REVELATION 17:1–18:8
PROVERBS 30:29–33

Today's reading in Revelation speaks of two things that are inevitable. First, the devil and his armies will wage war against the Lamb. We should not be surprised when we see the attempts of the darkness to overshadow Christ's light. But the second inevitable thing is that the Lamb shall overcome the powers of darkness. Always keep in mind that no matter how hotly the battles are raging, the end is sure.

These shall make war with the Lamb, and the Lamb shall overcome them: for he is Lord of lords, and King of kings: and they that are with him are called, and chosen, and faithful.

REVELATION 17:14

We are to be a voice for those who don't have one. We are to be the arms of Christ here on earth to reach out to those who are headed for destruction. We are to speak up against injustice. We are to judge righteously (without regard to social status, economic status, age, race, or gender) just as our heavenly Father does. We are to plead the cause of the poor and needy so that they do not get trampled on. How are you doing with all these things?

Open thy mouth for the dumb in the cause
of all such as are appointed to destruction.
Open thy mouth, judge righteously,
and plead the cause of the poor and needy.
PROVERBS 31:8—9

Day 364

MALACHI 1–2
REVELATION 19–20
PROVERBS 31:10–17

The robe of Christ was marred by the stain of blood as He rode forth into battle. Those who followed after Him, the heavenly armies, were clothed in perfectly clean and white linen. No spot of blood stained their robes. Your robe is perfectly white because He who stands next to you wears a robe that speaks of the bloody sacrifice that earned you your freedom. His bloodstains are your salvation and power. Follow Him into battle boldly, knowing that nothing can mar the white linen He has given you.

And he was clothed with a vesture dipped in blood: and his name is called The Word of God. And the armies which were in heaven followed him upon white horses, clothed in fine linen, white and clean.

REVELATION 19:13–14

God will wipe away every tear from your eye with the very hands that are scarred by the nails that were driven in the cross for your sins. Death will be vanquished for all eternity and slowly forgotten

as we live in blissful praise of our God, who conquered it for us. There will be no place for crying, sorrow, or pain as all things will finally be made right again. Could there be a more hopeful vision to hold on to in this life? Your struggles, pain, and tears are ephemeral and like a vapor that will be quickly forgotten in the all-encompassing light of God's glory. *Come, Lord Jesus, and make this future our present reality.*

Behold, the tabernacle of God is with men, and he will dwell with them, and they shall be his people, and God himself shall be with them, and be their God. And God shall wipe away all tears from their eyes; and there shall be no more death, neither sorrow, nor crying, neither shall there be any more pain: for the former things are passed away.
REVELATION 21:3–4

Scripture Index

OLD TESTAMENT